The Illusion of Due

First Edition Copyright © Jeffrey S Bardin ... . 71, LLC

Manufactured in the United States of America

1

The Illusion of Due Diligence

Being a security professional is a formidable career choice. To do it right you must take an oath of allegiance to your craft that is not welcome in the corporate world that ultimately employs you. The very credentials that make you marketable are, in the end, the very thing that can put you in the job market again and again. Taking ethical stands to live up to the code of the CISSP and the CISM takes courage, tenacity, thick skin and the willingness to walk away from an employer. Beyond this introduction are true stories of sex in the workplace, embezzlement threats of physical harm, impersonation of a federal officer, legal process abuses, complete incompetence, moral failure, just plain stupidity and more. Are you ready?

Understanding what you may face as a security professional can be valuable when the time comes to take an ethical stand or let the issue go by. Regulations have brought information security issues to the forefront expanding funding for technologies, staffing and training. More and more, however, we see exposure of data and leakage of sensitive information from industry giants like ChoicePoint and TJX. Do corporate boards and the C-Level management staff really understand what it takes to secure customer information? Are they more concerned with perceptions than resolving issues? What do you, the CISO, do when faced with legal consequences that can put you or others in jail? Can you even know unless you are placed in such a predicament? Surviving these situations can be quite stressful but there are ways to ensure your career remains viable when you choose to take a stand. Are you ready?

What do you do when ethical behavior, integrity, corporate due diligence and attorney client privilege collide in a cacophony of biased opinion and or negligence? How do you survive when you find yourself in the absolute middle of this vortex? The job of CISOs and CSOs is to protect corporate information assets while ensuring security obligations are met for the business. To ensure shareholders, investors, employees, customers and their interests are all protected. It is to provide the appropriate level of security for data and data transactions in preventing, detecting and responding to breaches. Security professionals live by a code of ethics, an ethos that demands correct action. Security professionals have been tasked with several duties; the duty to warn; the duty to disclose breaches to those who may be impacted; and, ultimately, the duty to survive, to live another day.

Security professionals are bound by multiple federal regulations and state laws that require diligence and competence in enhancing the security posture of the corporation that pays their salary. They are driven by risks, threats, vulnerabilities, controls, likelihood of occurrence of the threat, impact and residual risk. The greater the risk of harm, the higher the degree of care necessary to constitute due care (diligence). The stories you will read in this book are meant to help you answer the question "What do I do when placed in a potentially compromising position and how will I respond when faced with evasive, questionable and deceptive tactics that come from corporate leadership?" Are you ready?

Some readers of the draft of this book recommended I make it a purely academic endeavor. Some enjoyed it directly since it struck so close to home. Others felt I was taking advantage of my former employers since I was relating stories about them that were less than flattering. It is hard to align with such thinking (taking advantage of my employers) considering this is written without identifying anyone or any organization, and since those who feel this way have never been in the role of a CISO or working in like organizations. Regardless, some will find fault in the virtually redacted pages that follow.

In the end, I decided to publish the book with some modifications but with the original intent. What you will find as you read through the pages of this book are true situations that happened to me and with me as an active participant. At times I was fighting for my professional life as various cultural and organizational pressures attacked my position attempting to overrun my outpost before it was fully built. I do not see myself as a victim of any type but someone who has taken the journey that many of my peers have taken or are currently enduring. I hope that the many CISOs currently working in quiet desperation maintain their integrity when faced with illegal, immoral and unprofessional activities. What I intend to demonstrate in the following pages is the relative immaturity of the profession in the face of such well healed and established organizational icons that a CISO

4

The Illusion of Due Diligence

faces. I intend to show the general treachery we face from various positions of leadership and the insecurity many hold just under the surface of their public persona. It is my sincere hope that whoever reads this book learns from the experiences, errors and mistakes I have made in the past to further their own careers and the profession of information security, all the while keeping integrity at the top of the list of your personal and professional value system. At times it has been a tough row to hoe but to this point in my career, I have maintained my integrity with a relative modicum of honor required to keep my head held high.

In short, what do you do when:

- Employees are having sex on government property, video-tapping their activities, storing the results on government servers, using illegal operating system software, running a business from these servers and doing so while being paid with US tax dollars to do their real job.
- The internal legal team threatens to place your risk assessment information under attorney-client privilege.
- The CIO and COO are in therapy together.
- An employee is discovered impersonating a federal officer.
- You discover the CTO is embezzling money.
- Your boss is stealing hardware and selling it for cash.

The Illusion of Due Diligence

- The main internet-facing website terminates after running non-intrusive application vulnerability scans.
- Your boss, the CISO, continues to lie to the corporate audit committee and corporate officers.

What do you do when placed in such situations? How do you keep your job and maintain personal and professional integrity? Should someone go to jail? Do you violate your own ethical canons to protect yourself? Are you wanted for conspiracy for trying to commit security? ARE YOU READY?!

ABOUT THE AUTHOR

Jeff broke codes and ciphers and performed Arabic language translations serving in the United States Air Force (USAF) and at the National Security Agency (NSA), and also served as an Armored Scout Platoon Leader and Army Officer. He has worked in leadership positions in Fortune 1000 organizations. Jeff also has international experience in the greater Mediterranean region and the Kingdom of Saudi Arabia. He also has a BA in Special Studies, Middle East Studies and Arabic Language from Trinity College and a MS in Information Assurance from Norwich University.

Jeff was awarded the 2007 RSA Conference award for Excellence in the Field of Security Practices. The Bardin-led security team also won the 2007 SC Magazine Award for Best Security Team. Jeff has served as the CSO/CISO several firms and currently serves as the Vice President and Chief Security Officer for ITSolutions in Silver Spring, Maryland and maintains his own LLC – Treadstone 71. Jeff has published many articles, contributed to numerous books and sits on a number information security advisory boards and councils. Jeff holds CISSP, CISM and NSA IAM certifications and currently maintains a top secret clearance. Jeff can be reached via http://www.treadstone71.com.

The Illusion of Due Diligence

The Illusion of Due Diligence

Dedication and Thanks

I wish to thank my wife Nancy for persevering through the years of highs and lows. I could not have done it without you.

I also wish to thank my mother and father for instilling in me the concepts and requirements for personal and professional integrity as a core value for living life even though painful at the time of instillation

Lastly, I dedicate this book to the memory of Audry Lahue who lived a life of grace and integrity that is unsurpassed. In our home, she is remembered, sweet memories cling to her name. Those who loved her in life sincerely, still love her in death just the same.

Forward

When you see a photograph of a career soldier, their lapel tells a story. The awards and medals tell a lifetime's story of battles fought and victories won. With the ribbons, perhaps a purple heart for being wounded in action or *The Soldier's Medal* for distinguished heroism, the lapel tells it all.

Jeff Bardin is a career information security soldier. The battles he fought were not in the killing fields of faraway countries, rather in domestic data centers and in boardrooms with senior management. Looking at his coat lapel does not tell any story. But the pages of this book attest to the many security battles he has endured.

The Illusion of Due Diligence is not your typical information security read. If you are looking for 350 pages on how to install, configure and maintain a Check Point FireWall-1, with an additional 100 pages of screen prints, look elsewhere. *The Illusion of Due Diligence* is a firsthand look at the real skirmishes that information security professionals have to deal with, day after bloody day.

In the chapters of this fine book, Jeff lived the reality of what Professor Eugene Spafford of Purdue University observed that "If you have responsibility for security but have no authority to set rules or punish violators, your own role in the organization is to take the blame when something big goes wrong".

The Illusion of Due Diligence

Security professionals such as Jeff do their best to show management, who are far too often oblivious to the security and privacy risks, the basic due diligence they must do to bring their systems up to a most basic level of security. Rather than embracing such professionals and hearkening to their message; management often takes a Stockholm syndrome[1] approach.

Jeff's story is one that should be heard, as he is one of those who truly *gets* information security. Jeff gets security in the sense that he knows that all the firewalls in the world will not protect an organization from a malicious insider. He gets that unbreakable cryptography can be broken during the happy hour if management does not support effective processes around how they use cryptography. What Jeff gets about security, he has written about. And that message is something that today's management must read.

I had the privilege of sharing the stage with Jeff at the RSA 2010 Conference. From his talk, I came away with a lot. In *The Illusion of Due Diligence*, Jeff shares the stage with you, the reader.

---

[1] Stockholm syndrome is a term used to describe a paradoxical psychological phenomenon wherein hostages express adulation and have positive feelings towards their captors that appear irrational in light of the danger or risk endured by the victims.

The Illusion of Due Diligence

In *A Few Good Men*, Colonel Nathan R. Jessup challenged his adversary "You can't handle the truth!" For those that are looking for the information security truth, read on; if you can handle it.

Ben Rothke, CISSP, PCI QSA – Senior Security Consultant – British Telecom Global Services

Author of *Computer Security: 20 Things Every Employee Should Know* (McGraw-Hill)

The Illusion of Due Diligence

Introduction

Any resemblance to any persons living or dead is coincidental. The names have been changed to protect the guilty.

What do you do when ethical behavior, integrity, corporate due diligence and attorney client privilege collide in a cacophony of twisted opinions and institutionalized negligence? How do you survive when you find yourself in the absolute middle of this vortex? My job in the past has been to protect corporate information assets while ensuring security obligations are met for the business. To ensure shareholders, investors, employees, our customers and their interests are protected. It is to provide the appropriate level of security for data and data transactions in preventing, detecting and responding to breaches. As a security professional, I do in fact live by a code of ethics, an ethos that demands I do what is right. I've been tasked with several duties; the duty to warn; the duty to disclose breaches to those who may be impacted; and the duty to disclose the state of security readiness.

I am bound by multiple federal regulations and state laws that require my diligence and competence in enhancing the security posture of the corporation that pays my salary. I am driven by risks, threats, vulnerabilities, controls, likelihood of occurrence of the threat, impact and residual risk. The greater the risk of harm, the higher the degree of care necessary to constitute due care (diligence).

The Illusion of Due Diligence

Several federal regulations and state laws have been passed ensuring that public companies adhere to a set of rules that should be adopted into their IT governance models. Sarbanes-Oxley, Graham-Leach Bliley, HIPAA, SB1386, SB1633, Massachusetts 201 CMR 17 as well as the Minnesota law executed out of fear of another TJX. Considering this, you may think that most IT organizations and CIO's would insist on adopting many if not all of the strategies, standards, and guidelines brought forth in regulations and state laws. What you will see throughout this book is just the opposite. Human nature within corporate walls is morphed into an ugly byproduct of corporate greed and individual ego under the umbrella of perception management. I would have to say that not all organizations have gone this route but many have. The regulations and state laws have become just another set of guidelines that public companies use to obfuscate the truth behind the immaturity of their information technology organizations. In several of the companies I have worked, CIO's are intent on delivering software product on time and within budget at all costs turning a blind eye to the information security and privacy requirements embedded in these regulations and state laws. The corporate risk associated with these actions is enormous. The risk to the public, universal.

It amazes me that most CIOs do not thoroughly learn these regulations as they as officers of the company are beholden to them and are required to provide their signature indicating compliance on a periodic basis. It is equally amazing that other corporate officers including general counsel and internal audit fall in lockstep with the corporate line that is driven by dollars. The risks associated with managing costs versus those associated with communicated, exploitable vulnerabilities take precedence even though they are truly one in the same. What I have found is an institutionalized effort to manage the perceptions around IT organizations and in particular, information security ensuring that the illusion of due diligence is a corporate function and engrained into the fabric of the corporate culture.

ChoicePoint settled with several states providing $500,000 to the states to divvy up amongst themselves. For all its pain, Tennessee gets a huge number - $5,500.00. That half million-dollar number seems to be the going rate nowadays, but $500,000 for all states involved is a bargain for ChoicePoint. A mere 6 months after the initial announcement of ChoicePoint's breach, they were still sending sensitive information via email and Excel spreadsheets. I can attest to this since the data loss prevention (DLP) tools where I worked intercepted this traffic on a regular basis.

TJX and ChoicePoint along with all the others who have had publicized breaches is but the tip of the Titanic iceberg. Most companies are dodging bullets every day. It is my experienced opinion that more companies do not divulge breaches than those that do. Many believe it can never happen to them regardless of the amount of sensitive email that exits their borders on a daily basis. Once such company I worked for had a proven daily number that averaged to 3450 sensitive emails per day happily flowing out of the confines of their infrastructure. Identified to the C-level on more than one occasion, I took the final tact of issuing the CIO and CTO of this firm a business acceptance of risk form (BARF). Since they denied any and all safeguards and protection strategies surrounding this issue, I had to transfer the risk to them to get them to accept it as their own. It certainly is not owned by the CISO. My job is to identify the risks, provide mitigation strategies, plans, costs and prioritized roadmaps, not to accept the risk of the gaps found. The CIO as an officer of the company decided to ignore the BARF and chose to never sign it. The amusing thing about this situation was the fact that the CIO and CTO fully approved the BARF process. I guess they never expected to have one come their way. Regardless, the BARF made its way to internal audit and to some members of the risk management group where it was again shelved under the guise that our competitors were not safeguarding their sensitive outbound email and it would cause too much pain for external users to utilize 'any' of the proposed safeguards. This was a case of keeping pace with the Joneses? If they are not securing their environment, why should we? If our competitors are not doing it (regardless the risk to shareholders and issues related to regulatory violations), we are not going to do it either. The BARF contained multiple examples of competing companies using solutions of this type throughout their daily business practices. The whole idea of secure email was dead on arrival. Like lemmings at the precipice we jump?

The Illusion of Due Diligence

The current regulatory environment brings hope to the masses despite the fact that it has been years since the ChoicePoint exposure. There are currently bills in process that address these issues at a federal level. But since the federal government has not taken this issue seriously, nearly every state in the union has a separate bill of its own. You would think they would get together and craft a comprehensive bill considering they have had several years to do so. I believe the only reason we are seeing any activity in this space is not due to the actual exposures themselves but due to a regime shift in Washington. But it has been over a year since this shift and we still do not have a comprehensive federal law.

Before we go further, let's provide definitions to the vernacular at hand:

Ethics: The rules or standards governing the conduct of a person or the members of a profession. The study of the general nature of morals and of the specific moral choices to be made by a person; moral philosophy. A set of principles of right conduct.

Integrity: The quality of possessing and steadfastly adhering to high moral principles or professional standards.

Due Diligence: is the effort made by an ordinarily prudent or reasonable party to avoid harm to another party. Failure to make this effort is considered negligence.

Attorney-Client Privilege: Where legal advice of any kind is sought, from a professional legal advisor in his capacity as such, the communications relating to that purpose, made in confidence, by the client are permanently protected, from disclosure by himself or by his legal advisor, unless the protection is waived.

The Illusion of Due Diligence

(ISC)² and ISACA - Ethics

All information systems security professionals who are certified by (ISC)² recognize that such certification is a privilege that must be both earned and maintained. In support of this principle, all (ISC)² members are required to commit to fully support this Code of Ethics (the "Code"). (ISC)² members who intentionally or knowingly violate any provision of the Code will be subject to action by a peer review panel, which may result in the revocation of certification. (ISC2, 1996)

As a Certified Information Security Manager (CISM), I am bound by another set of principles as defined by ISACA. ISACA (www.isaca.org) is the non-profit organization that provides the most well know auditor certification. The ISACA® Code of Professional Ethics follows:

ISACA® sets forth this Code of Professional Ethics to guide the professional and personal conduct of members of the association and/or its certification holders.

Members and ISACA certification holders shall (ISACA, 2010):

Support the implementation of, and encourage compliance with, appropriate standards, procedures and controls for information systems.

Perform their duties with objectivity, due diligence and professional care, in accordance with professional standards and best practices.

Serve in the interest of stakeholders in a lawful and honest manner, while maintaining high standards of conduct and character, and not engage in acts discreditable to the profession.

Maintain the privacy and confidentiality of information obtained in the course of their duties unless disclosure is required by legal authority. Such information shall not be used for personal benefit or released to inappropriate parties.

Maintain competency in their respective fields and agree to undertake only those activities, which they can reasonably expect to complete with professional competence.

Inform appropriate parties of the results of work performed; revealing all significant facts known to them.

Support the professional education of stakeholders in enhancing their understanding of information systems security and control.

Failure to comply with this Code of Professional Ethics can result in an investigation into a member's, and/or certification holder's conduct and, ultimately, in disciplinary measures.

If you accept these definitions then we can proceed. Let's go back to the original question: What do you do when ethical behavior, integrity, corporate due diligence and attorney client privilege collide in a cacophony of opinion and negligence – and you are in the middle?

The Group W Bench (Guthrie, 1967)

The setting is the early years of 2000 while working as the security officer. There are multiple situations here but let's look at the amount and types of training we go through as required to support a contract of this type. In this case, there are a multitude of online training classes geared towards mischarging, sexual harassment, security and privacy, conflict of interest and a gamut of other courses required for completion each year that focus on confidentiality, integrity, and ethics. We were required to take this training on a yearly basis. 100% participation was required as a condition of the contract. The contractor (my employer) drove home the utter importance and requirement by all to complete these courses in a timely fashion. Failure to do so could lead to termination. Regardless of the contract wording, the corporation as a whole required these courses be taken as a condition of positive employment. The contract needed completion to check the box for potential bonus realization.

The contract was rife with political positioning and posturing. The new program manager was a hardnosed 'fixer' brought in to correct the course of this contract which was headed downhill like a speeding train with no brakes. In fact, a letter delivered by the agency to the contractor on Valentine's Day after the first several months of the contract became known as the St.

Valentine's Day Massacre since the ratings were in the low seventies, which for this company meant no contract bonus and that heads would certainly roll. The agency did not realize the gravity of what they had delivered. The fixer was brought in. I would grow to know him as "the Cleaner." In some circles, "the Cleaner" title is known as someone employed to take care of the dirty work at hand such as murders, intimidation, and the like. Our "Cleaner' was known for his no-nonsense approach. We soon found he was really a 'rule by intimidation and ridicule' type of leader (if you can call this a leadership type). His job was to improve the periodic ratings from the customer in order to secure millions in bonus dollars for performance. His own compensation hinged upon these ratings. Each functional group was individually rated and combined for an overall rating. Dollars were awarded based upon the ratings and the ratings were derived from specific measurements as defined and agreed upon during contract ratification.

During the first six months of my tenure on this contract, we had taken the security team to the top of the heap as we focused very closely on the contract requirements and metrics. The team was armed with very strong information security professionals in need of some leadership and guidance, which I was hired to provide. Our functional rating came in, in the low nineties. Overall the contract rated in the low eighties at the end of my first six months. A major improvement from the previous rating period, but still not enough for upper management. The next six months were deemed to be crucial for the contract as we would be whipped into performing at a higher level. My thoughts at the time were that if we all just focused on the contract requirements; became well schooled in every verb and adjective; then we would easily reach the Promised Land.

It was near the end of the subsequent rating period that the following incident would occur. As I said, political posturing was a daily staple on this contract. Internal lines were drawn and factional fighting occurred on a regular basis. I felt like I was in Beirut in the mid-eighties with Maronite fighting Amal fighting Druze fighting Hezbollah fighting the Izzies (Israelis).

We had recently procured a vulnerability scanning solution and were actively scanning the infrastructure for vulnerabilities. We ran into an anomaly that we could not initially verify. We asked some questions of the engineering group who seemed extremely happy to provide us with the necessary information. Like a convict confessing before final disposition (or better yet, the arsonist calling in the fire), the lead of the engineering group pointed us towards a couple of IP addresses that the scanner had picked up but could not scan. We traced the IP addresses to their physical location and found two servers located in an office far away from the power regulated and temperature controlled data center. After a bit of wrangling, we performed local scans of these two servers. What we found was quite exciting on the one hand yet extremely disturbing on the other. Per the requirements of the contract, we began to gather information off the two servers. Here is what we found:

Windows 2003 was running on both servers. Both versions had been evaluation copies of the software but the evaluation codes had been broken using a known cracking tool. Both copies were now unlimited license versions with no expiration dates.

Illegal copies of firewall software had been installed on each with rules specifically established to obfuscate any detection. Cracking security software really should not occur yet it continues today in other circles.

Firewall rules were created to allow by IP and name, access through the firewall to the two servers. Those named were few but were part of a warring faction. Dynamic IP allocation was required for all but a few within the organization. Those with static IPs need to be reviewed and approved by my group. This had not occurred. Having a static IP allowed one such conspirator to access the servers in question of f the internal network. We identified this as such since his full name was on the rule (an agent for the CIA he would not make).

The servers had not been patched or upgraded since inception. The servers were running anti-virus software that had been illegally acquired and loaded. The anti-virus software had not been updated with new engine or .dat files. Together the two servers had grown to 100 gigabytes of data. The data was production data, i.e., all server and desktop images were stored on these two servers.

Other support information was stored on these two servers and used in day-to-day activities accessed by contract employees throughout the country. One of the server administrators (part of another warring faction) was running a real estate business off one of the servers. All customer information including financials as well as home listings and email-snail mail distribution lists were stored there.

Word documents indicated an ongoing love affair between four contract employees with much of the illicit activity taking place in this office as evidenced by documented arguments over scheduled office use. Two of the employees were married at the time. There were rumors of actual video of sexual acts being performed amongst the four that was at one point stored on the servers in question. What we found where hints of this supported by still pictures of the various positions that could be added to either an x-rated Dilbert or a modern day Kama Sutra. We could not prove the existence of video although we tried "very diligently" to find any evidence of such in an effort to build our case.

Nevertheless, the still pictures provided enough evidence something of this type had occurred and proved to be a source of interest for quite some time. If only I had the presence of mind to charge for viewings!

When a husband of one of those partaking in the illicit activities came to visit the offices, we scrambled to physically remove him before any workplace violence incidents could be perpetrated. We were lucky since he left before any encounters. We were able to get his picture off the video security cameras, make copies and distribute them to all managers and front desk personnel. Regardless, he did penetrate the physical security of our offices and did roam throughout the office area eventually leaving of his own accord.

Keep in mind that computer crime is a felony violation of Section 1030 of the United States Code. Examples of computer crime are:

- Fraud achieved by the manipulation of computer records
- Spamming wherever outlawed completely or where regulations controlling it are violated
- Deliberate circumvention of computer security systems
- Unauthorized access to or modification of programs (see software cracking and hacking) data
- Intellectual property theft, including software piracy
- Industrial espionage by means of access to or theft of computer materials

- Identity theft where this is accomplished by use of fraudulent computer transactions
- Writing or spreading computer viruses or worms
- Salami slicing is the practice of stealing money repeatedly in extremely small quantities
- Denial-of-service attack, where company websites are flooded with service requests and their website is overloaded and either slowed or crashes completely
- Making and digitally distributing child pornography

Per the letter of the contract, we secured the two servers removing them from the network and moving them to a secure location, that being my office in another building. Here we started the task of forensically imaging the server since they had never been backed up in their nearly 20 months on the network. It is at this time that the beginning of what would become intense pressure began.

The deputy program manager was on the phone with me asking what had happened to these servers and under whose authority had I removed them from the network and physical location at the organizational headquarters.

Being the security officer for the contract, I was authorized to check hardware in and out of the headquarters' campus. I indicated they were secured in my locked office and that they were being forensically backed up. I also indicated that since they had never been backed up and that the imaging would be in-depth capturing all tracks of all sectors (and then some) on each hard drive. The whole process would eventually take nearly 4 days pending no issues. The issues we faced started out as cockpit error. The initial backup was not started in 'forensic' mode and therefore need to be restarted (after nearly 12 hours of activity).

As each day came, new pressures were mounted. The contract CTO decided to inform the organization CTO of the situation, unbeknownst to the program manager. I was called into a meeting with the program manager, deputy program manager and the functional manager who presided over the four people directly involved with the incident.

The three main characters here were the Program Manager who at one point professed to have put himself through college by selling drugs; the Deputy Program Manager who always had a cup of coffee in his hand with a cigarette not far off; and the Manager of the LAN Group who was sometimes know for very loud outbursts of rage.

They asked that I not deliver the news of the incident to the government until after this meeting had taken place (which by the way was not per contract requirements). It was already getting late with respect to informing my government counterparts. Regardless of the outcome of this meeting, my peers would be informed. This meeting was not to query on what was being found. They already knew what was going to be found. You see, the functional manager had approved the purchase of these servers 20 months prior to this meeting and had authorized their installation and operation in this office as a backdoor way to meeting operational goals without federal scrutiny and without the associated costs (again, another of the warring factions). This was one way to beat the system in his mind's eye. Despite the intentions, the operational goals were not met unless you consider running a commercial business from a customer's server and operational goal. If you do, then they exceed expectations. The Program Manager was more concerned with ratings impact and the Deputy Program Manager was just along for the ride.

The meeting started with my chair strategically positioned in a location under the direct gaze of the other three. It was obvious that they had been discussing the situation at length prior to the meeting start time. They had prepared their line of questioning and I would assume, felt confident they would achieve their desired results. Prior to the meeting, I was consumed with following the chain of custody and rules of evidence. I had the facilities staff change the lock on my door. The new lock did not work with the master key for that office area. In a defensive move, I acquired all keys to my door. The master key for this location would not work on the new lock. I documented each and every step and move with time hacks and precision. The overall report was not as yet completed but my next step, per contract requirements, was to inform my counterpart (the customer) with an initial report of the incident, which by the way, was a contract metric that could derail the bonus. The irony is quite clear.

I came to the meeting armed with the initial draft report complete with screen shots of all bulleted items mentioned above. This was the Alice's Restaurant version of an information security investigation, i.e., twenty-seven eight-by-ten color glossy photographs with circles and arrows and a paragraph on the back of each one explaining what each one was to be used as evidence against *them*. I was supposed to be the Officer Obie (Guthrie, A Tribute To Officer Obie, 1969) of this investigation but in fact was the Arlo on the group 'W' bench. I distributed the evidence to the three interrogators and we began the dance. I was questioned on several fronts:

> How did I become aware of this situation?
> Where were the servers?
> Who do you think you are taking these servers without our knowledge?
> Why would you take these servers?
> Are you sure we have to do this?
> Do you know that these are production servers that are critical to our efforts here?
> What do you intend to do with the servers?

What do you think you are going to do with the information you have?

Do you realize what this will do to the contract and this period's ratings?

Why do you have to report this again, please re-explain?

What will be in the final report?

Who are you going to inform?

Do you realize that we knew nothing about these servers?

Did we ask you this yet? (Are you sure we have to do this?)

Are you on a witch hunt here?

Can you prove everything you have presented?

What will you do to fix the situation?

When are you presenting this to your counterpart? How will he take this and what will he do?

Why do we really have to inform the government on this situation?

Aren't you being a bit overbearing in taking those servers?

We need them back in production right away. When can we get them back?

Tell me again, why do we need to document this?

I think you get the picture. This meeting occurred in the morning of day two. I indicated that by the end of day two, I was going to call my federal counterpart and inform him of the situation, that we as a contract were already late in providing initial notification of the incident. I was also going to follow up that call with an email version of the initial draft report. We proceeded to review the draft report. There were no redlines as the report was objective in nature and content as required. The facts were stated and evidence provided. Of note, two of the four involved in this incident had left the company one week prior to the discovery of these servers. It is apparent to me that the warring factions had reached an impasse and new, more severe battles had been and were taking place in the shadows. My role was that of a pawn for one and an enemy for the other, by definition of the security officer position which I occupied.

That afternoon, I called my counterpart from the secure confines of my office. He was initially stunned at the incident as I covered the salient parts. I sent the draft report to him before ending the conversation (PDF format which prevented modification). He indicated he would review the report and get back to me by noon the next day. With the imaging of the two servers still running, I secured my office and left with my laptop for the evening (along with secure electronic copies of all pertinent data).

The next day brought a new round of questioning and inquisition. It was evident that someone had attempted to access my office after I had left the previous evening based upon the line of questioning. Without coming out and saying they had tried to enter my office, the Deputy Program Manager and Program Manager queried on the status of the servers (by phone) and were soon at my door to view the situation. I noticed an interest in the doorknob by the Program Manager as he directly worked the handle and examined with intent the lock. It was only for a short moment but the intent was there.

Based upon the imaging information, the process would take another 24 plus hours to complete. I had sent an email and voicemail to them both after the contact with my federal counterpart the night before with a brief overview of the conversation. They were obviously anxious for an initial ruling from the customer.

At about two in the afternoon, I received a phone call from my federal counterpart. He was relaying two questions two me:

When will the servers be back online?
How will you prevent this from happening again?

I indicated that the imaging would be complete within a day but that all software must be legal and that the Program Manager had agreed to purchase all necessary software (minus the firewall). As new keys for the software became available, the servers would be placed within the data center and entered into the normal patch management and backup cycles. As for how to prevent this from occurring again, my thoughts wandered off to how I would really want to prevent this versus what I was allowed to do. Should I have the power and facilities, I would terminate all associated with the incident and replace them with those instilled with moral fortitude and a sense of right and wrong. I would perform a traditional communist purge with those responsible sent to a gulag along with their families, if they were allowed to live at all. At the very least, lie detector tests with an ethical bent would be administered to those in line for the positions. Anyone not passing the tests would be sent for re-education. In actuality, we had drafted a plan to perform more frequent vulnerability scans and network mappings as well as periodic announced and unannounced physical reviews of contractor accessible offices within any/all customer facilities.

For this situation, it was clear that both the contractor and the customer did not want a public flogging over the incident. Even though the evidence was clear, concise and indisputable, no disciplinary action was ever taken against those involved or against the contractor. A question that still vexes me is: Should I have reported this to appropriate legal authorities? This was not a contract requirement and reporting of this type was not specified. It was in fact the responsibility of my counterpart. The felonies committed would be swept under the rug and the incident forgotten. It is not the job of the security officer to pass judgment but to gather the evidence per procedure and report the evidence as found. We did that and secured the imaged hard drives in a safe as required by contract. Other copies may have been made of the data as methods of protection and self-preservation but that is just speculation.

We turned the servers back over to the LAN Admin Group so they could upgrade the software per the findings and plan, entering them back into production

Situational Review

Even though we did not find the devices for quite some time and we needed to be given a hint or two, we were able to follow the rules of evidence and chain of custody of the servers and subsequently the forensically copied hard drives. The security team performed well in acquiring the devices. Reporting (at least on paper) was detailed and definite with proper evidence collected that identified the suspects adequately to stand up in court.

What did not work well was the ability to detect the devices located in an office versus the data center. Network access control (NAC) was not available but we could have used capabilities with the switches and the asset management database. MAC addresses of all assets could be stored in a flat file; each device plugged into the network scanned for its MAC address and compared to the definitive listing from the asset management database. If the MAC address does not match one in the list, access is terminated. This method can also determine physical location of the device. It is a poor man's NAC using Perl but it does work. The process of reporting should have been expedited. Speed in notifying our counterparts was hampered by program manager perception management and fear mongering as well as 'just under the surface' threats to my employ.

My first step should have been too quickly, verbally notify my counterpart that an incident had occurred relative to unauthorized devices on the network with the investigation just starting. Followed up with periodic status reports and I may have been able to diffuse the confrontations with the program manager and his henchmen. Then again, they would have been perturbed that I informed the customer of the issues without proper vetting and review, i.e., either way would have garnered their wrath.

Additionally, a more concerted effort at security awareness focusing on incident response directed at education contract employees at all levels may have given me a stronger foothold and base from which to operate. Had they known contract details relative to incidents including processes and procedures outlined in discussions and solidified with sand table exercises and practiced, then as with most any information security issue, expectations would have been set ahead of time. Security awareness can be used on multiple levels and with multiple approaches to educate your immediate management so there are no surprises. They must be made to fully understand the ramifications of action and inaction. It could be reasoned that had I armed the program manager and all senior staff with a full understanding of incident handling, whether advertent or inadvertent actions, then the execution of the process should have gone off like clockwork. Keep that in mind as you mature your security program.

Shaken Not Stirred
18 USC 912 (TRAC, 2009)

Whoever falsely assumes or pretends to be an officer or employee acting under the authority of the United States or any department, agency or officer thereof, and acts as such, or in such pretended character demands or obtains any money, paper, document, or thing of value, shall be fined under this title or imprisoned not more than three years, or both.

Impersonation and sexual harassment are not normal investigative tasks of an information security officer but does in fact show that the path towards physical security and information security convergence is finally coming. What do you do though when asked by the head of human resources to gather information concerning such activities? With respect to this alleged activity, I chose to partake in the investigation following standards for rules of evidence and chain of custody. It began with a phone call one evening from a direct report of the contract program manager. The call came in while sitting quietly watching a less than engrossing TV show, laptop already fired up reading the day's news on CNN while hitting the blogosphere. The manager, let's call him Ted, had a sense of urgency in his tone. I knew right away that something was wrong, my mind taking me to an intrusion, malicious outbreak or hack of some type. But the conversation led to a very different situation. Apparently, one of his staff had been out with some other employees that evening partaking in food and merriment. His employee, let's call him Bart, had allegedly been making overt attempts to seduce one of the women in the party. Not unusual for a man (although inappropriate) after imbibing some alcohol, but the advances were not welcome. So, why is this situation unlike most any night at the bar?

After multiple repeated attempts to entice our heroine (let's call her Amanda) to leave the bar and come back with him to his hotel room, Bart decided to up the ante with inner secrets that no women could resist. Bart was secretly hired by the program manager on a mission to infiltrate some unsavory elements within the contract and within the customer's organization. His role was to seek out those acting on behalf of some outside organization (most likely an evil competitor) or even THRUSH (Technological Hierarchy for the Removal of Undesirables and the Subjugation of Humanity), identify the structure of those who had penetrated the contract and customer's organization, and become part of their trusted inner circle. As a deep cover operative, Bart would be able to take down the whole apparatus putting his own person in harm's way. Bart, obviously a highly trained professional, was not at liberty to disclose the true details of his extremely dangerous mission. He chose to disclose only enough to entice the target of this evenings affection to swoon over his station while keeping in confidence the real intent of his job on this contract. Bart even went so far as to present a federal officer's badge, flashing it quickly in the dim light of the crowded bar hoping to stimulate the required hormones in our heroine should the transmission of his highly alluring pheromones not do the job. Assured of the night's conquest, Bart proceeded to press the matter to the point of physical contact placing his hands on the leg and thigh of Amanda. Our heroine proved to be much more sophisticated than Bart had bargained for removing Bart's hand from her silky thigh and directly rejecting his advances. Undaunted by this clear attempt to extend the game (not end it), Bart shuffled his chair ever closer to Amanda. He placed his arm around the back of the chair of Amanda letting his hand slide to the uncovered shoulder.

The show was over. Amanda firmly removed his hand and uttered loudly and clearly that she was not interested in any uncertain terms. She quickly removed herself from the bar calling Ted to inform him of Bart's violation of sexual harassment standards as defined by corporate policy and as clearly delivered through required trainings and testing. Amanda called Ted since Bart was a direct report. It was obviously clear that the sexual harassment training all were required to take on an annual basis did not take. The policies though were well articulated and clear; zero tolerance. Why would I get the call? Let's rewind about three months when the story really started.

Ted was in need of a very senior network engineer to complete his team and fulfill the responsibilities of his given objectives. Expanded work on the contract forced

Ted to begin a search for the right person of skill and integrity. I say integrity because Ted demanded it and also due to standard background investigation requirements that would be sure to discover any activities that did not meet the requirements of this position within the government. The skill requirement was due to the level of effort and expertise for a senior network engineer; one who can architect full solutions as well as build them. The résumés started to flow and the vetting process came in parallel. During this process, unbeknownst to anyone, the program manager had re-contacted an old workmate living in the Tampa, Florida area. I say re-contacted as they must have remained in contact over the years with phone numbers and locations. The workmate had actually been the program manager's administrative assistant while on contract at a location in England. It is hard to say if there was ever any relationship other than professional between the two but it is clear that their bond was tight. Rumor has it that the admin assistant and the program manager had been paramours. The administrative assistant have moved to the Tampa area and somewhere in the mix, married into the military. The fine gentlemen she decided to spend her days with was Bart.

As it would turn out, Bart was a network engineer. His resume quickly appeared in the pile of those to call and qualify. In fact, it was quickly moved to the top ensuring Ted would see it. Ted was informed to give this person a good look in no uncertain terms. Ted's staff had begun the screening process and narrowed the field down to what was believed to be highly qualified candidates with all the prerequisite certifications and experience. Bart's résumé did not read anywhere nearly as strong but they would be good soldiers and screen this candidate.

Unanimously, Ted's staff all rejected Bart after the phone screen. He did not have the skill; he did not have the experience; he was not qualified. The short list of candidates was presented to human resources and ultimately to the program manager. Ted was summoned to the program manager's office for a closed-door conversation. You can imagine the conversation; innocent enough in its tone yet just under the initial layer of conversation was the real intent. We have all had these conversations with those above us. Whether over a hire, a hardware/software purchase or selection of vendor; they tend to appear when you want them the least and when the selection is extremely critical. Ted attempted to present his case that due to the highly technical requirements of the position, someone with impeccable credentials need be selected. Ted explained that the contract would benefit from such a hire if done correctly that would most likely translate into contract enhancements and higher periodic ratings, which would in turn lead to a higher overall bonus. Undaunted, the program manager pressed his case for Bart and impressed upon Ted that he should, as the networking team manager, ensure improved contract ratings regardless the hire since his understanding was that Ted was the best in the business. I always love these conversations salted with underlying intent and peppered with strokes of the ego that at best were insincere. Ted left the office knowing he had no choice but to bring Bart in for a face-to-face interview. It was clear that the program manager was damn determined to ensure that Bart was going to be hired. In fact, Ted knew that he should just cut to the chase and present an offer to Bart. But to do so would mean two things: that Ted would not maintain his own personal and professional integrity which his team would recognize and; that the program manager, being a cagey veteran of such activities, would not allow a hitch in the process, that Ted would need to go through all the standard hiring criteria even though the future outcome was known. To not follow the protocols would lead to suspicion and bring scrutiny to the process. It would lead to potentially illegal activity.

Bart and two other candidates were brought in for the interviews. Ted and his staff along with human resources would perform the three to four hour interviews over a two-day period with recommendations to come at the end.

He flew in at company expense for the interview. During the interview process, the program manager decided to spend some time with Bart. Keep in mind that the program manager had never met Bart in the past. Bart was the only candidate selected for this lunchtime honor. Soon after the interviews, Ted presented his chosen candidate to human resources. Of course this was rejected and Ted was again summoned for a discussion with the program manager. The rejection was not the decision of the HR Manager but at the instruction of the program manager. Ensuring his staff knew of the selection and the meeting, Ted proceeded down the hallway for another education in cronyism as well as self-preservation.

Part of the new hire process is the background check. Standard for any position of trust as required by this contract. An outside organization would perform the background investigation taking data from the required forms that needed to be completed. It was learned that Bart was actually unemployed at the time and had been unable to find work in the Tampa area. He had worked for a large telecommunications provider but for some reason, had lost the job. It was not due to a reduction in force, an upgrade with immediate effect or due to revenue issues with the telecom provider. It was one of those terminations that neither the company nor the former employee would confirm as a termination but an amicable parting that was best for both parties. This was the type of termination that became legally sealed by agreement and signature. We would never know why Bart left this position. Like discharge papers and the DD214[2] in the military there should be a coding system for reasons for termination in the commercial space. Although no reference would be given by Bart's former firm as a matter of policy, don't you think there is some

---

[2] DD Form 214 are military discharge papers that includes type of separation, character of service, authority and reason for separation, separation and reenlistment eligibility codes.

level of responsibility and accountability companies need exhibit when someone is terminated for cause? Apparently not.

It was known on the contract that moves of new hires from one location to that of the contract were no longer allowed. I found this out when I had been offered the top security slot. Out of work myself and struggling to keep financially afloat with periodic contracts for training, risk assessments and penetration tests, a fully funded move was just what the doctor ordered. I asked for such as part of the new hire agreement but was informed that no one received moves and this position was no different. Disappointed to say the least, I accepted this over no job at all and proceeded to fund the move of my four bedroom home and family of four nearly 700 miles to the south all-the-while traveling back and forth; staying in hotels; and feeding myself (no easy chore).

Bart was hired in as a network engineer. A small victory for Ted in that he did not have to place Bart in the senior slot which would further alienate his already demoralized staff. Regardless, Bart was provided a fully funded move from the Tampa area, a thousand miles to the north. A fully funded move includes flights to and from your home of record; hotel stays of up to sixty days; all meals and expenses paid including car rental and to top it off, a per diem over and above meals and expenses. Normally a package reserved for a manager slot and above (like the top security position), Bart made it known that he had received this package. Much to the ire and utter disgust of many including myself, Bart was sure to point out his importance and relationship with the program manager much like a made man in the Cosa Nostra.

Fast rewinding to 'Why did I get the call?' we now have a better picture of the situation as a whole. I was contacted as a trusted advisor with the expectation that I would know or could find out specific information. Ted also knew of my own personal situation relative to the move and was playing on that nerve. He expected I would jump at the chance to 'burn' Bart. Believe me, the temptation was great but I resisted stooping to the level of a Bart and giving into my own underlying emotional desires to terminate with extreme prejudice. Maintaining objectivity and only participating where appropriate and where asked was key to living up to the standards of the security certifications I hold and the ethos behind them. I explained to Ted that investigating an impersonation charge, much less one for sexual harassment was not the responsibilities of my office although I would begin the process. I did provide Ted with 18 USC 912 explaining the contents. I then directed Ted to human resources indicating this is where the investigation should originate. Should human resources request support, they would need to formally engage the services of the security team. Ted indicated he would work through human resources. I also provided human resources with all details to date of the situation.

A full investigation was performed by human resources staff and a corporate resource not directly assigned to this contract. Let's discuss this corporate resource. Most ombudsmen within this corporation reported into corporate human resources. This being a contract, there would be little if any conflict of interest with such an organizational structure. Of all the several divisions of this huge conglomerate, ours was the only one where the ombudsman and responsibilities thereof reported directly to the division vice president. Control was the order of the day. Suppression of activities unbecoming to the letter of the contract was institutionalized. The investigation took a short five days and the finding was inconclusive. Amanda felt betrayed and helpless. Human resources were instructed to follow the final report findings to the letter of the law and Ted was to continue with work as usual. Bart felt both exonerated as well as persecuted. He professed his innocence on the sexual harassment charge even to the point of leveling counter charges. If you knew Amanda you would understand how completely absurd this was. Bart did not push the issue hoping the issue would quietly go away after his initial outbursts of persecution. At a later date and in confidence Bart admitted to flashing a badge but would never produce it. He wore this like a badge of honor. Somewhere in the background of this whole affair was the program manager manipulating the scene like a puppet master. The human resource manager intimated that Bart had attended a closed door meeting with the program manager to discuss the situations. Having an office directly next door to the program manager was advantageous for human resources. She confirmed the meeting and provided confirmation as to the tone and decibel level of the program manager's voice. In keeping with Bart's true mission on the contract, the meeting was to be a daylight clandestine operation, one that never took place (even though it did). The program manager, known for his appetite for chewing up and spitting out staff made it clear to Bart that his behavior was unacceptable. To most, this was both an admission of guilt as well as complicity in a corporate cover-up. It would be bad form for the program manager to have used his influence to hire a less than perfect network manager. Being wrong was something not tolerated by the program manager. Regardless of the issue, situation, project and/or outcome, the program manager had a knack for directing blame to the location and person within his radar at that particular time even if that person was not directly related to the issue. With a direct resemblance to the pointy-haired boss and a man's equivalent to Brittany Spear's voice, the program manager would direct his ire with the accuracy of a scud missile on a moonless night in the Nafud Desert[3] causing indiscriminate casualties with his carpet bombing style of corrective action. He believed that improvements were directly proportional to the number of duplicate reports his staff was required to produce monthly. The more reports we produced with the same information the better off we would be, come review time.

---

[3] A desert in the northern part of the Arabian Peninsula known for sudden violent winds and crescent shaped sand dunes

Somewhere along the timeframe of the investigation into Bart's activities, the agency was informed of his alleged activities. An investigator from the outside investigative agency scheduled several meetings with contract staff to collect information and reach a decision. As both a direct and indirect participant in the activities, I was subpoenaed to provide an affidavit as to my knowledge of Bart's actions. Most of the data I provided was that of hearsay since the impersonation and sexual harassment charges were not something I could have experienced firsthand. Throughout the interviewed I continued to direct the investigator to the human resources manager who performed the investigation and to the ombudsman. I provided information but stressed that even though this information was well known throughout the contract, that I had no firsthand knowledge and could not confirm nor validate its authenticity. It was apparent that the investigator was not happy with our conversation but it was the truth. That was the last I heard of the investigation (at least for this timeframe).

Still singed by the knowledge that Bart had received a full move and reminded daily by my ever-present recurring credit card statements, I grew ever more disgusted with my boss, the program manager. I hadn't realized that I could summon so many levels of disgust. Like a radiometer that tracks the amount of radiation over time, my complete disdain for this person grew with each encounter. Regardless, I maintained my integrity and objective focus leading the security team to high levels of performance. We led all functional groups on the contract with the highest ratings three periods running with increases each period. The security team had helped pull the contract up by the bootstraps to a level of bonus equal to several million dollars. We were praised by the customer for our professionalism, execution and operational excellence. During our periodic reviews, the contract specified that overviews and metrics be aggregated and delivered. Using specific security metrics, charts, graphs, and correlated events demonstrating measurable security posture improvements, I delivered a presentation that wowed the customer. This would prove to be the last time I was allowed to submit a presentation of such caliber. I was instructed to 'dumb down' the presentation since several of my peers and program manager lackeys could not deliver to the same level of competence. The security team was looking too good relative to the other functional groups in particular the desktop and server Tier 2 and 3 groups. Needless to say, we received few accolades and no financial rewards for our efforts from the contract. Mediocrity was rewarded. This was the first time that I understood that mediocrity was the new crème that had risen to the top.

Back to Bart. Like anyone of Bart's makeup, sooner or later they will revert to old habits and bring unwanted attention their way. Bart had selected and purchased a home in a nearby state due to significant price differences. He traveled some sixty minutes each way (on good days). Bart found that if he arrived early to work, the only person at work prior to his arrival would be yours truly. He also discovered that if he left 1 to 2 hours earlier than required, he could make the trip home in a scant 40 minutes on his newly purchased Harley Davidson, money received from his sign-on bonus.

Since our offices were located in a different building from that of the customer's, Bart learned he could schedule fictitious meetings there for 2:30 or 3 in the afternoon. He would leave the confines of his cube and head directly home. Our security policy required complete logoff of customer machines at the end of each day. Bart would perform this task with gusto as the event logs on his PC would eventually reveal.

About a month passed when I received a formal request from human resources to examine Bart's PC event logs. Ted had asked me to do so but I required formal written requests for such activities and the concurrence from human resources. I assigned the task to my best investigator and over a period of two weeks, diligently collected, aggregated and delivered these logs to human resources. A suggestion was made to review physical access logs since proximity card access was required to the office space. A like request was made of the customer, which never materialized since their system had had a problem during the times requested (another story, another time).

The data collected seemed to be sufficient for disciplinary action, but as you know, interpreting the data for potential sanctions is not the responsibility of the security officer. Our responsibility is to follow the rules of evidence and chain of custody in such matters ensuring the evidence is not tainted. During our data collection efforts, we learned that Bart was monitoring our monitoring of his logon and logoff times. He grew suspicious that he was being watched and approached me on the subject. With an air of wrongful persecution, Bart strode into my office. I heard him coming as he sauntered down the hallway like a bull in a cage just before release into the corral. He asked me who was logging into his PC every night. He asked if it was one of my staff and why we would do such a thing. He wanted to know who authorized this activity. My approach in dealing with Bart was to explain the responsibilities of my office. In appealing to his true mission on the contract, I informed Bart that any investigation the security team may be tasked with performing must be kept confidential. As he would fully understand, disclosure of any such activities and even acknowledgement of their existence would compromise the investigation. Such activities were not to be taken lightly. If he felt that there was some wrong doing occurring that was targeted towards him, he should immediately report it to HR. Bart left the office obviously unsatisfied with the answers he received. Determined to escalate the situation, Bart played his next card in this game, that being a meeting with the program manager. Being that Bart was on the contract for undercover purposes he should have known what my response would have been.

Ted learned of the meeting with the program manager during a shouting match with Bart over Bart's inability to work a full eight hour day. Ted knew it was time to present all evidence through HR to both the program manager and once again to the division ombudsman.

Let me ask you this question: What is the definition of insanity? Performing the same task over and over again expecting a different, positive outcome. Ted and the HR manager clearly documented multiple counts of mischarging (another one of those required and tracked corporate training courses as dictated by all federal contracts) presenting their findings up the ladder. True to form, the program manager went into action to squash the data and hide the infractions. Bart was again called in from the cold for another round of verbal spankings, which was the extent of the punishment. The division ombudsman was never heard from and all discussions surrounding this proven offense were stricken from all annals of the contract. Like the Teflon Don, Bart escaped the persecutions through his relationship with the program manager acting as both judge and jury. Ted was admonished for his efforts in doing the right thing and the head of HR on the contract was summarily verbally disciplined for performing her job.

Three years removed from this contract, I received a call from the outside investigative body on both my work phone and on my personal cell. It's funny how they tend to get your private number without much effort. Another investigator claiming to be performing a survey on investigations within the scope of this organization wished to go over the facts and associated with the 'Bart' investigations. We spent nearly an hour covering all the data. It took me a few minutes to recall the whole situation but as the questions came, the data began to restore from gray matter tape. The original investigator had written that I would not cooperate indicating that I could not speak to the details of the investigations. I explained that that was not the case; that I was at least two people removed from the allegations and could only refer to them as hearsay. Without proper firsthand knowledge, I would not and could not articulate a position. I did though explain that after the investigation, we had gathered more evidence on mischarging that was conclusive and factual, but I again directed the investigator to the HR manager who had since left for another position within the corporation, and to the network manager who was still working on this contract. All data that had been collected while performing the job as the security officer had been turned over to my predecessor and to HR. I also provided the name of the investigator from my former team as I knew he had not gone far, having taken a job directly with the customer. I knew this was karma man and that justice would be served. Bart would receive his due and the program manager had previously received his when terminated from the contract for cause.

Situational Review

The ability to gather information both through discussions and interviews as well as through virtual methods worked very well. Processes and procedures were very well defined and detailed making the execution relatively effortless. Having skilled staff was also quite a plus as the requirement for staff education was little.

What did not work was the dependence on people to do the right thing. Isn't that always the case? One of the themes of this book and in fact for most of my career has been the inability of those in positions of authority above me and to my sides to act with honesty and integrity. Even though we gathered all the appropriate information in the appropriate format delivering it to the appropriate internal authorities, it was dead on arrival.

We could have taken this information outside of the firm and pressed the situation based upon the law and US code. Allowing outside authorities to handle the issue may have been the right way to go. I think many in the information security profession fear this approach due to horror stories from others or the whistle blower tag that could then be applied to your name and reputation.

In Case of Emergency, Break Glass

When starting out in any new field as a relative newcomer, I have found that you tend to fight very hard to keep your job. At least for me and based upon the location, an area where jobs are few and far between, maintaining your job was tantamount to survival. The second shift job was initially challenging for about the first couple of months. Just enough time to understand the job requirements and operational activities needed to execute at an optimal level.

My boss, we'll call him Don, at the time was said to have his favorites and I was warned of this since being on the other side of the favorites game could be detrimental to your longevity. He had been with the firm for nearly 18 years becoming fully entrenched in the politics that proved to be his saving.

It was not long before we disagreed on a few operational and performance items. Like all positions for any employee, the desire is to have a career path that is well defined and attainable. It is here that we did not see eye-to-eye. Don did not see potential in my abilities. I on the other hand was just asking for opportunities to make my own way within the structure of the organization. The firm was a Fortune 50 firm that had several mechanisms in place should you be aware of them and know the proper procedures for using these tools for upward mobility. I spent a great deal of time learning of these through some contacts in human resources. Otherwise, one might never know of their existence. Not having a background in computer science, I also leveraged the corporate tuition reimbursement program taking Basic, Pascal, C, Advanced C, Data Structures, and Systems Analysis and Design. Believe me, coding was not my forte as I was more akin to breaking codes than writing code. In order to grow within the information technology department, I exerted great effort to quickly learn.

Don took into account these efforts but offered no support to assist in the growth of my career. The tension grew to a one-time, hallway shouting match. I don't remember the triggers for the intense disagreement nor do I remember particularly what was said. I do know that I placed myself solidly on weak ground having had such a disagreement with a senior manager. Many of my peers secretly agreed with me and directed me to human resources ensuring I reported the incident, assured that Don would be on the same path.

One of my friends in accounting, let's call her Kathy, saw me heading into the office of my favorite human resources rep. After completely relaying the account of the shouting match, I left the office only to be questioned by Kathy as to what was going on. I gave her the short version of the situation whereby she nodded her concurrence that I would now have a very difficult time surviving and that Don would be sure to build a case for my rapid departure. Kathy invited me back to her desk, whispering as to something of interest that could help me maintain my employment. We spent at least 15 minutes discussing the deep secret on Don's activities she had held close for several years. I photocopied some documents she had stored away and made off with my insurance package. Break glass only in case of emergency.

A few months passed and the always tenuous relationship with Don only spiraled further into a hostile work environment. Don made every attempt to force my resignation from the threat of shift change to the midnight shift to lost paperwork for tuition reimbursement to rejecting vacation requests to requiring unrealistic delivery dates on projects to changing requirements without communication of their change to monitoring my every coming and going to reviewing every piece of work provided for any potential issue or problem. This continued for another several weeks.

One evening after a particularly ugly meeting with Don in which he accused me of not correctly scheduling mainframe production jobs, which by the way was not something I ever did as it was assigned to day shift personnel, I felt a sense that something was about to hit. My office was two doors down from Don's. As dinner time came, I decided to venture into Don's office to see if there was something there that would either confirm or allay my fears. I was not sure what I was looking for or really why, but in I went. Was this the right thing to do?

Was I breaching an ethical tenet? Was I acting with complete integrity or was fear driving my actions?

Upon entering Don's office I found lying on the circular table, a copy of phone bills that looked very familiar. Familiar because the numbers were that of my home 30 miles to the north. Being a relative newlywed I tended to call home once a night. Keep in mind that this was before the days of email, instant messaging and cell phones. These ubiquitous tools of present day were merely a gleam in some engineer's eye. My wife worked days leaving before I got out of bed and going to bed before I returned home. This led to my calling home on a nightly basis to ensure the weekend schedule for newlywed activities was booked on course.

The calls were usually no more than 5 minutes and I knew it was against policy to use the business phone since it was in one of the corporate human resources handbooks. I also knew that most everyone ignored this policy seeing employees and managers alike making long distance phone calls on a daily basis that were not job related.

Fear grew from my stomach to all extremities as I knew that Don would use this policy violation to execute his plan. This would be my downfall. I clearly violated the policy as written. For the next two hours I paced the aisles, sweating as I racked my brain on how to proceed. How could I explain the phone usage? What would I do without a job? How would we pay the mortgage and where would I be able to get another job? Fear turned to despair until I remembered my insurance policy. Should I use it? What if I was wrong? What did I have to lose? I decided to break the glass.

With much trepidation I placed another phone call only this one was to Don. We would have our 'final' confrontation. Don would be requested for an evening meeting with his favorite employee. It took me two hours to summon the courage. I wrestled in my head what I would say and how I would position it. I placed the call. I indicated that we needed to speak right away that it was very important that we discuss some items concerning my employment. I believe he thought I was about to submit my resignation based upon his quick response at saying he would be there within 15 minutes. What was about to be presented was far from my resignation, but a defining moment for his career and mine.

Don arrived close to 9PM. We were the only two in the office of the IT shop. He strode into the room with a sly small as was his way and asked to get straight to the point. I prepared some words for this conversation during the past two hours of nervous anticipation but conveniently forgot each and every one. I asked Don why he wanted so badly to fire me. He responded that he had a dislike for my behavior, my performance and did not think I had what it took to be part of his organization. He indicated, that I was not following corporate policy and I would suffer for this. We did not go further down that road as I preempted his conversation with an interruption. It went something like this:

"I'm not the only one who has not been following corporate policy. In fact, I believe you have violated several policies over the years that could be seen as criminal." His whole face grew red with the initial onset of an anger I had not as yet seen in Don. I continued. "It seems as though you removed old pieces of computer hardware from the building, signing all the proper property passes and documentation. It seems the pretense was to sell this old equipment on behalf of the company, only the company has never seen one penny of this money and you have not returned any of the hardware. As a matter of fact, folks in finance are quite curious as to where the money has actually gone. It looks to me like some level of embezzlement, which I am sure, violates some sort of corporate policy." His face was now absorbed with the glow of red mixed with purple as if about to explode. He started to approach me as if to attack. Don noticed my posture had changed as well. I stood firm, prepared for anything, expecting a physical altercation, fists clenched. Don stopped dead in his tracks as the realization found its mark. His face quickly went from one of anger to disbelief that this unworthy employee who he was about to terminate had maneuvered to a position of strength. One can only imagine what went through his mind at that time. He began to ask me how I had learned of this but quickly stopped. I believe he understood that this was his admission of guilt and ceased to proceed with this or any line of questioning. We quickly concluded our evening conversation and Don left for home.

As I sat in my chair, I realized how utterly exhausted I was. The evening's activities had taken its toll on me as the sweat dried on the back of my neck and the telltale circles began to fade from my underarms. I wasn't quite sure what to expect when the dust had settled. I had protected my position within the company knowing I would never make another long-distance phone call. Self preservation is a strong motivator. The encounter could have gone negatively for me but in this case, the evidenced was accurate and secure at my home. Don would never treat me with disdain again. As a matter of fact, he decided to take a position six months later with another division and move his family out of state to do so. He kept his home and apartments ensuring they were all rented. There were rumors after his departure that he was flying back and forth at the corporations' expense, while deducting all travel and expenses on his income tax as a business expense for his rental apartments. Double dipping of this type could be seen as fraud if in fact true. I chose to ignore the rumors and move beyond Don.

Within a year after this event I was presented with two different corporate awards for exemplary performance and customer service. The awards sit in my cabinet at home as a reminder of the struggles pre and post Don and the opportunities afforded me once the roadblocks had been removed. I never did learn of what happened to the phone records but suffice to say they never surfaced.

What I did was not necessarily following the tenets and mores of my current position. You may judge this at the very least as a character flaw or bad behavior. I look at it as a moment in my career that I would not repeat. I would follow the straight and narrow and not compromise my position. Making the phone calls due to the hunger pangs of love was not justification for policy violations that could lead to termination. Although tempted, I did cease this activity. What would you have done in such a situation? Would you have taken this information and delivered it to human resources seeking Don's termination? What would that have done to Kathy in accounting who knew of his activities for several years? Would you have had the fortitude to have that evening meeting? I ask this knowing that this question will elicit several different responses. Look deep into your psyche and examine your personality. Ethical issues surround this event on many levels. How would you have behaved on this fateful night had you been in the same shoes? If I was a true security professional at that time, which I was not, would I have behaved in such a manner? This was early on in my career with my office still located in the data center (next to the Halon).

Situational Review

The ability to summon the courage to confront Don was effective and did produce the desired results for that moment in time although I should have turned this information into the corporate ombudsman immediately upon receipt. Don would have been under the pressures of corporate legal and most likely terminated for cause. With Don terminated, my life would have been much easier at work. There is a good chance I could have grown professionally much faster with new leadership. Would I have then stopped making the phone calls home? Human nature says no.

Building relationships throughout the corporation provide me the information and insurance policy that solidified my employment. You can never underestimate the importance and power of relationships and the network it affords you. It is absolutely required to build sincere relationships where give and take is the order of the day. These relationships provide useful information and intelligence at several levels. Do not betray the trust of your relationships keeping the need for ethical behavior and integrity at the forefront. Networks of this type can propel you onto a new position if leveraged correctly.

We all face managers who maintain a tight circle of trust around them. Breaking into this inner circle needs to be analyzed based upon ethical values balanced with corporate survival. You must though maintain integrity over loyalty. Survival instincts may tell you to bend if not break your own value system in order to become part of the pack. Tread carefully here as you need to be able to look yourself in the mirror each and every day. Making it to the inner circle is not always best although the instant gratification and protection you receive ensures personal survivability, at least for the duration of this regime. Regime change can result in a purge.

Ellsworth Toohey[4]

The Dotcom era was upon us like a thunderbolt. Deciding to leave the confines of brick and mortar corporate America, I found myself working for a 100+ year old firm looking to extend its lifespan with a foray into a startup. With revenue on hand, $25 million in the bank from the company's primary lender and promises for another $25 million along with tax increment financing (TIF) from the city as well as another $5 to $10 million in angel and private investments to flood us should the TIF come to fruition, I felt comfortable that this effort could make the grade although I did have doubts that would later prove correct. I'll not discuss the particulars of the business other than it was truly a next generation effort having learned at a previous startup how not to go about this effort.

As an officer of the company, I attended board meetings and high-level meetings with my peers tasked with protecting the shareholders amongst other responsibilities. My peers in this case were the CFO, the

---

[4] Ellsworth Monkton Toohey, who writes a popular art criticism column in the Ayn Rand novel, The Fontainhead, is Howard Roark's antagonist. Toohey is an unabashed collectivist and Rand's personification of evil (when speaking freely, he explicitly compares himself to Goethe's Devil, who tempted Faust to destruction). Toohey represents the stifling, decadent forces of Communalism and Socialism. His biggest threat is the strength of the individual spirit enshrined in Howard Roark. He falsely styles himself as representative of the will of the masses.

COO, and the VP of Human Resources as we all reported in to the CEO. Originally, I had reported to the COO but the CEO in a shift of responsibilities wanted the CIO reporting directly to him. It was at this time that the rift between the CEO who will be named Dan, and the COO who will be named Ellsworth became readily apparent.

For the next several months, Ellsworth was seen to be posturing for the CEO position. One small problem here: the position was already occupied. Meetings with the board were for the most part uneventful. The board had difficulty understanding the concepts of the startup, but was fully behind it. Entrenched in the old business, which by the way was generating revenue and would continue to do so, they were largely concerned with the progress of the build and of course the numbers. Good men all of them with the best intentions at heart, they fully supported the CEO and his drive to take his company to the next level.

One fateful day in September we watched with horror from the 40 inch screens in our network operations center the crashing of two jets into the World Trade Center. My wife and I had scheduled lunch together for this day. We met still stunned at the attacks. We discussed what would happen next believing that I would somehow be recalled or slapped into federal indentured servitude. What we didn't see coming was the speed of the eventual demise of the startup and the disturbing events that would lead up to our final days.

As a team, we prepared our documentation for the final application of the promised $25 million. The TIF had gone through its paces and we were assured it was going to happen. A 15-year TIF meant millions in savings as long as we met the letter and spirit of the agreement staffing up to 40 new people at an average salary above that of most in the city. New revenues would have a very positive impact on the community and the state as a whole. We had periodic meetings with the governor and attended media covered press conferences with both the governor and other dignitaries. The world was our oyster and we were about to see it slip from our grasp.

The funding source decided that with economic indicators all pointing downward; with 9/11 impacting our national psyche and shaking the economic base, we were no longer a safe bet. Phone calls and trips to meet with representatives of the funding source continued for a few weeks. Ultimately, we were only able to secure $5 million in additional funding. This would impact the TIF. The TIF agreement specified the $25 million as a requirement. The angel funding specified the TIF and the $25 million as requirements. The private funding specified the angel funding, the TIF and the $25 million as requirements. The house of cards was about to collapse. We began to scramble looking for another $20 million in funding. The business plan was honed and rebuilt several times in efforts to package our limited intellectual property for each different venture capitalist organization. Each presentation was met with a firm no.

We looked at our business plan and began to think outside the box. What other things could we do? We made several efforts to return certain equipment and software that was costing us a hefty monthly sum. The lease on one of our buildings was signed for 40 years. Exploration into this lease started what would be some very unusual findings.

The lease was negotiated by Ellsworth, our COO and a lawyer registered with the state as a practicing lawyer. Not only was Ellsworth a practicing lawyer, but he had been part of a prestigious firm with a focus on mergers and acquisitions. Ellsworth was a nervous guy who struggled to ensure that everyone liked him when in fact very few did. It was clear that his purpose as the COO was twofold; ensure that he was the focal point of the firm both internally and externally and to take control of the company ousting the locally born and bred CEO. One incident involving Ellsworth with a few of those who basked in his glow surrounded fine wine. Claiming to be a connoisseur of wine, a few folks decided to replace the Concannon Petite Syrah with TJ Swann during one evening of food and drink. As was his way, Ellsworth went through the motions of the wine tasting ritual before anyone could partake in this fine libation. After a few sniffs and a couple of short sips, the TJ Swann was proclaimed to be a semi-sweet, fully bodied wine that would be quite appropriate for this evenings affair and one of the best that had crossed his refined lips in recent months. The shell and outward phony persona that protected a damaged personal psyche was at the core of all his corporate dealings as we would see. His personality would flow back and forth from the yin and yang. His need to be the center of attention along with his need to be liked and overtly negative and attacking nature towards anyone who disagreed with him or was in his way demonstrated an inner turmoil that we were all about to experience firsthand.

Ellsworth, as with most people had some skills of value. He was very adept at working the legal framework and the parties involved for the most optimal solution. Most optimal for his and the law firms client and for the law firm themselves. Ellsworth had worked the 40-year lease deal with a local businessman. Struck before I had started as the CIO, it was assumed that with his extensive background in negotiations and mergers and acquisitions, that Ellsworth would extract the most favorable terms for the company. The terms of the lease were in fact very favorable for the building owner. A 40 year, no termination lease with an interest rate that was very high for the period of time was executed. One would have thought that Ellsworth was working for the business owner. I questioned how such a contract made it through CEO and board approval. Apparently, Ellsworth never presented all the details of the lease until after contract ratification. Even then, it was presented as a well-negotiated contract for the company. Maybe it was one of those "trust me" type of conversations that you have with a senior member of the company knowing that they must have the company's best intentions in mind and that they are the most qualified person to perform the negotiations. Regardless, the CEO and his team should have vetted the contract prior to submission to the board of directors for final ratification. I would question how it made it through the process with the board since at least one lawyer was a member. The bottom line was obvious: We were paying much more than necessary on a contract based upon our 100% success in this venture. A forty-year lease? A bit ludicrous. I think a 5 year lease with opt out options would have been sufficient.

Ellsworth began to schedule meetings with financial brokers and firms hired to find us funding. One such firm we will call Granite, held a meeting with the CEO and his direct reports. We examined the overview documents Granite provided looking at the terms that required a relatively high down payment with no guarantee of success. In addition, Granite wanted a significant stake in the company along with other payments should the funding come through.

On a parallel tract, Ellsworth had learned of and contacted some local businessmen who had been successful in startups before. We didn't know much about these gentlemen but decided to follow Ellsworth's lead for the meeting. What did we have to lose?

The meeting was held at our offices and included the CEO and his direct reports. Two gentlemen attended and represented themselves as a corporation we will call Dough. It was obvious after an hour or so that one of the gentlemen was the financial source and the other a self-proclaimed startup specialist who passed himself off as a highly respected CEO who could turn any situation around given the proper support. It was also obvious that there had been several conversations between Ellsworth and Dough prior to this meeting. They were in synch on several topics and were working to an as yet unknown agenda.

Overall, we agreed the discussions went well and we would continue at a to-be-determined date within the next week. This is where the subterfuge started to become visible.

During the past couple of years, the COO had been slowly positioning himself as the face of the company and the next CEO. Only problem was that the current CEO had no intentions of moving on. Ellsworth was always the face to the press. He had negotiated the TIF. He had pushed for and was granted several meetings with the governor of the state. The CEO was always in tow but was not presented as the face or brains of the operation. Ellsworth had brought in a well-respected marketing executive known for her marketing prowess and contacts in the New York City area. We will call her Doris. Doris had put together a marketing plan that was based upon New York style budgets and constituency. The program was well thought out; well documented and included both strategic and tactical aspects. Should the plan have been developed for a tier one market, it would have been perfect. Doris had also worked quite an arrangement for her son working several hours away in a farmhouse tucked away in a bucolic neighborhood of a New England state. Her son was authoring all the articles that Ellsworth would place his name upon and publish in regional trade magazines, local newspapers and online media outlets. His articles were well developed and delivered but overall very high level without significant depth or foresight, something I thought was required for a next generation effort as we were positioning our product suite. As the CIO, I wanted more control over these articles and indicated that I should be driving these articles and in fact, authoring them. This would not only save the company consulting dollars but deliver the message direct from the source. At the time of my discovering that Ellsworth was not authoring these articles, I was still not aware of the identity of the true author.

The arrangement demonstrated the nepotism and cronyism apparent within this firm. Doris' son was paid a monthly stipend of four thousand dollars for these monthly articles averaging 800 to 1000 words per edition. What Ellsworth received was industry notoriety and name recognition that hid his mile-wide and inch-deep knowledge which became his mantra that we heard on a daily basis as cavorted with external clients, local government officials and potential business partners. Ellsworth's job was to ensure the stipends continued. As soon as I learned of this arrangement, I began efforts to remove this costly contract from the organization and began writing the articles myself establishing relationships with the same outlets previously used. In addition, the articles (not to boast but as a statement of fact) were more cutting edge and provided more technical and business depth relative to what our true corporate mission was.

My push into this role created quite a ripple. Doris was extremely upset with the new arrangement and made it clear to Ellsworth. Ellsworth approached me (this was prior to the beginning of our financial downfall) to communicate Doris' displeasure. I defended my position. Why pay someone outside the firm to write articles about our technical direction when I was charged with setting that direction and could author the articles very closely to our plan without an extra four thousand dollars a month? Regardless, I pressed on and began to author articles for publication ensuring they had proper review and validation prior to publication.

At a meeting with the CFO one fine summer day, I replayed the meeting with Ellsworth on the authoring of articles. A wry smile came over the face of the CFO. He chuckled as he explained to me that the 'gentlemen in the country' was none other than Doris' son. He further explained that he was being paid a hefty monthly sum for these articles. He welcomed this change of events and as an officer of the company and architect of the product suite, I should in fact be driving the message. This change would save the firm several thousand dollars a month. I queried further on how such an arrangement could be established without examination from the board. He indicated that Ellsworth was given carte blanche over marketing activities and it was largely a 'black hole.' The CFO also indicated that several product and marketing staff were hired from Ellsworth's previous positions and that they had neither the technology background nor proper qualifications. I pressed further asking how Doris would be allowed to establish such a contract since it could be considered a conflict and how Ellsworth would allow this. Doris it was discovered was not an employee of the firm but was being paid $10k per month plus expenses for her part time work. I stress part time since Doris would come and go at her pleasure working usually around 3 days per week in total hours. Mind you, Doris knew her stuff but for that fee plus expenses and the extra for her son posed some questions that need be asked and answered. Why were we allowing such an arrangement and who structured this deal? Of course you know the answer but I ask, "Where was the CEO during the process?"

Doris had many contacts in the industry and it was through her contacts that we were able to reach the governor of the state. This did not come without a cost as Doris sourced to another vendor to lobby the governor for both access and influence. I never saw either the paperwork or fees associated with this second sourcing arrangement but based upon what I did know about Doris, I'm sure it was not for pocket change.

Two weeks passed without any further meetings with Granite or Dough. Suffice to say that I became a bit disturbed that these meetings were not on our docket considering our financial situation. Through some light investigative work, and discussions with our VP of HR, I learned that the meetings had in fact occurred but only with Ellsworth and a couple of his minions. Ellsworth had positioned himself with Granite as the heir apparent for the throne. If he could provide the funding that would save the company, presenting this to the board, he would be able to execute a swift and effective coup d'état. Ellsworth had secretly been working a separate business plan holding meetings with Granite. The CFO, VP of HR and I thought that Granite was brought in due to research performed by Ellsworth from prior contacts in the marketplace. With the same bit of naiveté previously exhibited, we assumed his intentions to be above board and in line with those of a corporate officer. Further investigation found that the dynamic duo from Dough had recommended Granite in exchange for high-level positions in the new regime. Dough would occupy two seats; those being COO and another C-level position with an undetermined title, mostly acting as a silent partner. Ellsworth would be anointed the new CEO and the current would be dispatched with the swiftness of a clandestine, midnight raid. Granite would get their fees and ownership; the CFO and VP of HR would be brought in (or not) and yours truly would face a take it or leave it type fate.

If the plan was discovered by the CEO, it would be immediate grounds for termination and legal action. An old fashion coup was being planned in the face of potential corporate financial ruin. I decided to confront Ellsworth on his secret activities.

The morning after the discovery, I forced a meeting with Ellsworth. Entering his office, I closed the door without comment and sat in the chair directly across from his desk. Angry at the current state of affairs, I found it quite difficult to contain my emotions. Knowing it was the only way to have a civil conversation; I maintained proper decorum and started the line of questioning. Ellsworth was quite convincing in his answers but his posture was clearly defensive in nature. I posed the line of questioning in such a way as to indicate little knowledge of his clandestine activities with Granite and Dough. His answers eloquently packaged. He appealed to my awareness of the CEO's shortcoming stressing that during unusual times, definitive action needed to be taken to preserve the company. The current CEO was not the man to lead us out of the current situation. He would only drive us further into the abyss of ruin. Although Ellsworth may have been correct in his assessment, his intentions were less than honorable. Further to, he was clearly violating his contract as an officer of the company. He was conspiring with outside forces to take over both the startup and the one hundred plus year old firm. As a means to an end, he found no ethical issues with his actions. It was clear in his mind that this was the only course of action to take. The gears were in motion and he needed my allegiance to add another piece to the puzzle. He stated how happy he was that I came to him with these questions that he was about to include me in the conversations as it was time for me to learn of the palace coup. As a respected knight of the round table, my sword was needed to enact the justice necessary to dethrone the CEO. The plan was well in motion; where did I stand?

Another meeting with Dough was scheduled for that afternoon at a hotel located directly across the street from our offices. The following night, a previously scheduled meeting with the CEO and his direct reports was on tap and to be held at our corporate law firms' boardroom just down the street. I would use this time to expose the plot but needed more information and detail in order to fully derail Ellsworth's underhanded plans. Without pledging my allegiance to Ellsworth and his band of raiders, I indicated I would be in attendance for the hotel meeting.

I walked into the meeting with Dough setting next to Ellsworth and Ned, another of Ellsworth's handpicked staff aligned with him. The CFO had also been invited to this meeting but had very little knowledge of the content.

Let's digress and examine the background of Dough. These gentlemen had roots in another state with summer homes in the general area. The financial wizard of Dough had made his millions in retail, specifically in the fast food restaurant business. He decided to tell us all at the start of this meeting in order to adequately impress us of his financial acumen and prowess. In fact, he was very active in securing the franchise rights for his multi-state area of influence for another such blockbuster concept surrounding pizza. He was about to open a line of 'cook your own' pizza stores. The idea was to make-to-order and have on hand special-made pizzas that people would pick up and take home to cook. The store would also cook onsite for an extra fee but the clincher here was the unique concept of we build it, you cook it. Amazed as I was at the ingenious nature of his new mega-millions project, I didn't see how this would fly in light of the multitude of pizza outlets from various local and national chains in the area already, much less the already available frozen pizzas at your local grocer. He was sure the concept would take hold and he could retire within a couple of years. I prayed he would not ask my opinion of his new venture. Being honest to a fault in such cases, I was prepared by nature to let him know how asinine the project sounded especially opening such a chain in a down economy in a New England state far away from a major metropolitan area and without the type of clientele I believed he needed. Proud and smug, he sat posed to take advantage of our situation most likely seeing our operation as ripe for the plucking. The other half of the Dough duo was also a man of means. They had a business plan for a business such as ours and had already started operations across town. For their services, a peak at their plan, an opportunity to join forces with their business, and an opportunity at securing $10 million dollars, we only needed to come up with $800 large and deliver it to Dough within the next 30 days. Dough provided their technology business plan to us at the meeting. I quickly scoured the pages looking for the intellectual property and hook they eluded too.

After nearly 15 minutes of scanning, I came to the conclusion that Dough had nary a clue as to what they were trying to do. In fact, their financials required $10 million to get the project off the ground. They had self funded up to this point and had some products and services on the street already, having secretly opened their doors a scant ten miles up the road. The eight hundred thousand we were to provide was not an entrance fee but in fact, was the money they needed to keep their venture afloat long enough to secure another $10 million. Instead of being someone who would fund our soon-to-be broke venture, Dough was itself about to go south for the winter. How this project would work was with $800k from our coffers, Ellsworth would secure the CEO slot; Doughboy number one the COO slot and Doughboy number two would be able to continue his quest as the number one cook-your-own pizza king of New England. Granite had already provided some funding to Dough and Dough needed our $800k to not only keep Granite interested but to get their self-funded dollars out of the project. It seemed as Dough knew both their technology venture and ours were certain to fail. They were looking for a patsy and obviously felt they had found one with Ellsworth and our venture. We came to understand this plot when the CFO and I began asking very pointed questions on the business plan, solution sets and funding sources. The Doughboys saw their mark and we were it. The solution sets as stated in their business plan were tired and targeted towards the mom and pop space. There was no way they could execute and they knew it. Their operation down the road was about to collapse and they wanted their money out. Ellsworth, blinded by the sheen of the throne reflecting off his own ego, could not see their misguided intent. He was prepared to go forward and execute the plan. That was why the CFO was invited. I was there to take this fine plan and develop the solution sets. Feigning an outside call on my cell, I left the room and placed a call to the CFO. He answered whereby I asked him to leave and meet me at the Starbucks on the corner. We met and discussed the contents of the meeting. He too was thoroughly amazed and disgusted. Ellsworth was going off the deep end. The stress of failure had worn away the thin veneer of this exterior personality. We had a glimpse of his true essence. The view was not pleasant. We decided to present our findings at the staff meeting the following night.

I made myself invisible during the day leading up to the staff meeting. I gathered and documented as much as I could of the events leading up to this day relative to Granite, Dough and Ellsworth. I performed online free and paid searches on the Doughboys and Granite. Nothing of real value came of these searches but I felt I had my historical data in order. I also examined the business plan and website of their technology venture. In my opinion, with a glut of like-businesses already dotting the electronic landscape, Dough was about to be overcooked.

I arrived early to the meeting. Being late fall the sun was setting to the southwest early in the evening. Armed with a strong coffee, my laptop and a strong sense to do the right thing, I sat in wait as all began to arrive. The CEO was chipper but tense. The CFO sat at the end of the table kitty-corner from my seat. Ellsworth arrived and true to form, occupied the head of the table. The table was easily fifteen feet in length having seen many a board meeting and heard many a secret divulged in other such meetings. After the VP of HR arrived, we began the meeting.

It did not take long for the fireworks to start. Ellsworth quickly turned his conversation to a blame-ridden diatribe against the CEO. Every misstep, every miscalculation and every lost dollar lay squarely at the feet of the CEO. He went on for about ten minutes directing his attacks towards the CEO. The CEO was clearly unfit to lead and unfit to continue leading this organization. Ellsworth struck to the core of the CEO's position lambasting him with a well-prepared monolog complete with various epithets and expletives. With each passing moment he gained confidence in the silence of the room. He was executing to plan about to call for a vote of no confidence. This was soon to change.

The CEO slammed his fist on the dark wood of the table a loud crack echoing down the hallway. He arose staring directly at Ellsworth and let go a barrage of verbal punches that shook the room. His face red with anger, he blurted out how it was not he who was unfit but Ellsworth; Ellsworth who had crafted and executed so many worthless contracts that made the company liable for years to come. If only the CEO knew the real story behind Ellsworth's contempt. The CEO decided to call a break in the meeting to cool off. He apologized repeatedly as we took a break from the meeting. I decided at that point that it was my turn to enter the fray.

During the break I was able to speak with the VP of HR. She expressed her complete disgust as to what had just occurred. Her anger, directed as it should be, was towards Ellsworth. She was appalled at his behavior. She was unaware of Ellsworth's real intentions but she had her suspicions as to where his actions would lead us. She felt that it was time for Ellsworth to resign. That his true colors were showing during a time of extreme stress. He could not be trusted and the board should know of his action. I took this opportunity to explain the events over recent days as they applied to Ellsworth, Granite and the Doughboys. She could only shake her head in disbelief. The meeting reconvened.

The CEO again apologized for his actions. As he was about to apologize again, I politely interrupted, asking if I could have the floor. He concurred. I stood from my chair and began to describe the recent actions relative to Granite and the Doughboys. Continuing, I ensured all knew I did not concur with the actions and was not initially included in the plot but brought in only after some cursory investigations and a forced face-to-face with Ellsworth. I directly admonished Ellsworth for his conduct defining it as detrimental to the stockholders and completely out of line with decorum for an officer of the company. Ellsworth knew where I was taking this conversation. He was not about to let me utter another syllable. He sprang from his chair shouting in anger at the preposterous nature of my comments proclaiming that this meeting was a waste of time and we were all wrong to accept the current course of action. His hands flailing and saliva flying, Ellsworth proceeded to stomp out of the room spraying epithets as he exited. His infamous borrowed saying 'I'm a mile wide and an inch deep" would never be truer on multiple levels. Shaming us all for our unified position, he strode from the room with false righteous indignation. We all sat for a moment in silence. I pondered how the bubble had finally burst for Ellsworth. The man who would be king was reduced to fits of anger and outbursts of juvenile behavior. Any chance of replacing the current regime was gone.

One final sidebar on this whole situation that I was soon to discover was the weekly counseling meetings. The VP of HR replayed for me several months of counseling that Ellsworth and the CEO had attended. Due to their intense inability to get along, the CEO and the COO of this venture were undergoing what amounted to marriage counseling. Their relationship was strained. The counseling, as the story goes, found that Ellsworth had a deep seeded need for approval largely due to his ineffective relationship with his father. Both Ellsworth and the CEO, rated as passive aggressive by the counselor, had difficulty in clearly and openly communicating, especially with anyone who was direct especially during times of stress and duress. When informed of this counseling, I sat stunned in the VP of Human Resources office contemplating how the number 1 and 2 leaders of the company were in therapy with one another. This could only be true and not something that was made up. The makings of a sitcom, yet I had lived it. The split was inevitable.

Suffice to say, Ellsworth was not summarily removed in a timely fashion. He was allowed to stay on until the bitter end continuing his attacks against the CEO although somewhat muted. He took his severance in a lump sum eventually landing a position with a one of the larger firms in the area with national ties. I eventually had direct knowledge of his activities at the new firm. His behavior did not change much as he was continuing to stir the pot and work the politics. People like Ellsworth need to be avoided at all costs. People like Ellsworth are users.

Situational Review

Well, I must admit that not a whole lot worked very well in the situations encountered during the stint at this company. The system to remove subversives at high levels did not work at all. I believe it would have been more effective to notify the CEO and board in a closed session of Ellsworth's activities early on in the process versus waiting for a C-level meeting to communicate the issues. I should have insisted on his termination for cause and immediate dismissal for his conduct as he obviously violated the code of conduct. His gross disregard for his position as an officer of the company and all subsequent responsibilities under the auspices of his office could even have led to legal action against him. He attempted to subvert the company for his own personal purposes. His actions were contrary to someone of his post but then again, we have repeatedly seen people in such positions continue to violate the law and the trust of stockholders. This should not have been a surprise but when you are part of the mix, you get to see the ugliness up close and personal. It makes you feel unclean.

Did Ellsworth get a cut from the 40-year lease? Was he making monies on the side by virtue of his position? I think not in both cases but I will never know. Nor do I care to. It is something I don't need to dredge up and relive.

I'm not sure that insisting on his termination would have worked since the CEO and COO were in marriage counseling together already. The fact that you have the two senior-most people in counseling is absolutely astonishing. Relationship counseling is the process of counseling the parties of a relationship in an effort to recognize and to better manage or reconcile troublesome differences and repeated patterns of distress. The COO should have been divorced early on and a new person brought on with the appropriate skill, personality and corporate culture match. If something is in a state of stress, remove the source of the stress. Occasionally officer relationships get 'strained', which means that they are not functioning at the optimum extent. There are many possible reasons for this, including ego, arrogance, jealousy, anger, greed, etc. Often it is an interaction between two or more factors, and frequently it is not just one of the people who are involved that exhibits such traits. Regardless, what was demonstrated for several months was a combination of ego, arrogance, jealousy, anger, greed, envy, and overt deceit. Not really a healthy combination conducive for any company much less a fledgling startup.

Ellsworth's own personal experiment with the company was over. He had lost in his efforts to overthrow the CEO. I am certain his rule would have been termed despotism. In power a new cult of personality would flourish as long as all paid homage.
With Ellsworth gone, would we have signed a 40-year lease? Would we have paid $14k per month to one

family for part time work (3 days a week at best)? Would the poor decisions on technology purchases occurred and the free spending without results and controls taken place? I can only say that my attempts to return much of the technology acquired was thwarted under the banner of 'losing face' as the governor of this state had a direct hand in the efforts. All efforts to return the hardware and software purchased were for naught. I was not part of these purchases having arrived after-the-fact but having just left a firm where 'if you build it they will come' did not work, I was acutely aware of the issues we could and did face. This was not hindsight but experience drawn from all too familiar mental scars still healing. What is quite ironic is the fact that later in my career I would briefly work for one of the companies we attempted to return the technology to; another unsavory organization that is known for eating it's young.

Keep Your Friends Close - Keep Your Enemies Closer

At one point in my life, I had my own company. Multiple personality tests over the years indicated a propensity for such a challenge. In fact, while at one Fortune 500 firm, I was given three options to take for my future: 1- Change your personality (which you cannot) or you will not succeed here; 2 – The Company will change (which it cannot) or you will not succeed here; 3 – Leave the company and start your own. When given such a read on your future with a firm where up to that point you have been successful, is an invitation to move on. Any other option would be an exercise in futility and a suppression of creative spirit.

There was a particular series of incidents while running my own firm that further eroded my trust in human nature and people in general, which continues its downhill run with increased velocity today. We were truly the only security firm in this state at the time and the time was such that no one was buying security services since they did not realize they needed them and regulations were not driving them as yet (even today they don't secure what they need and even though the regulations are clear, they are ignored like a lesion that turns into a malignant tumor only addressing the disease when it is too late). Breaches were occurring but no one even knew they were occurring. Whenever you have to educate someone or some entity on the need for something, getting them to then purchase what you are selling is inherently difficult; the sales cycle is very long. The fact that some believe you have to sell security is a misnomer. It is all about risk and they own it. Give it to them in manageable parts that they can handle with Cadillac, Chevy and Yugo options advising them on the best option but letting them choose (documenting every step of the process).

When you let someone into your office to review potential partnership activities, the expectation is that there is some level of personal and professional integrity that guides those involved to act and behave with proper form. When further bound by a non-disclosure agreement that specifically outlines this behavior, the expectation jumps to a higher level of perceived integrity. In my years of experience, NDAs are about as valuable as the paper they are written on (much like the stock options of the year 2000 and 2001 and the thin slices of paper found in restaurant bathrooms). A formality for entry to your intellectual property.

The situation I am about to describe takes place at my office with a potential partner or competitor who is looking to break into the security consulting business. She has been traveling around the world on a sailboat for the past year and decided during this voyage that her vast experience in Microsoft training and the training gained from securing the dingy to the sailboat qualifies her as an expert to offer information security services. What would she believe otherwise?

Shame on me for not recognizing that the overwhelming drive to succeed coupled with a demonstrated lack of integrity makes a recipe for unscrupulous behavior. Anyway, back to my office. Ariel, as she will be named, decides to reach out to me signing the NDA and asking to visit my office for a powwow on how we could potentially work together. The initial conversation goes swimmingly. I offer her coffee which she accepts. I venture off to the other room to pour the already made coffee. As I return to the office, obviously entering earlier than expected, I find Ariel furiously writing down all the book titles and authors of the pertinent books located directly to her right in the bookcases. I had not been out of the office but two minutes. Recognizing that she has been caught, Ariel quickly and adeptly indicated that she had been looking for a particular book that she identified in the bookcase. She had forgotten the name and therefore did not wish to forget it again and decided to write down the title and author. This of course did not explain the list of other books on her pad that I happened to view upon re-entering the room.

The conversation lasted another 15 minutes during which I grew increasingly angry and disgusted. This engagement would turn out to be just the beginning of wonderful relationship with Ariel built from the beginning on deceit. My anger was at myself for allowing my inherent initial trust of people to get the best of me. Why is it that I must seek the best in people knowing that most I have met in this business don't give a damn about integrity but have economics as their underlying principle that is all-powerful and to be worshipped?

So why do you say did I continue to attempt to build a relationship with Ariel? For the most part, I would have to say I try to find the good in people during all early encounters. My thoughts here as I venture back into the gray-matter archives, turn to an inherent albeit sometimes naïve condition I have to trust people out of the box.

The meetings with Ariel continued. We discussed bidding together on a state contract for security training services. My first instinct was not to go forward with this venture and I should have listened to this gut feeling, but alas I chose to give Ariel the benefit of the doubt and jointly author the proposal for this contract. We will come back to this effort momentarily. Our company website had been up for some time, articles published in regional technology trade magazines both paper and online, and relationships established with various legal, government and healthcare organizations. The website contained the usual service and product offerings along with a plethora of links to information security and IT governance resources. Information about the company including biographies on corporate officers was published on the site. Over coffee one morning while reviewing a newly released press release on HIPAA security services, I decided to take a look at Ariel's website as I had not reviewed it in some time and was awaiting an email from Ariel to review the partnership site and our corporate information and logo. I found the site easily and began to methodically review each page to understand her message.

Like molten lava rising up through every available avenue of the volcano, the visceral reaction I had to a few of the pages nearly caused me to throw the cup of coffee through the office window (luckily it was open). Verbatim and without even the grammar correction I had been planning to change was a page taken directly from my company's website. My first instinct was to get in the car and with extreme prejudice and malice aforethought, venture over to Ariel's office. Instead, I began to use a tool to fully copy and download her entire website. While downloading the site, I continued to scour the site for more copyright violations.

Another page included information on her corporate management. What struck me as a bit odd was the name on the top of the browser of the web page. It was the name of one of my partners in our company. I looked further throughout the page finding exact sentences on skills of her staff taken directly from my partner's bio. More in-depth examination found course offerings taken directly from our website. What would be my next move?

After discussing the situation with one of my partners, we decided to contact a lawyer he knew who was locally known for tenacity in the courtroom. After providing evidence and some brief discussions, a letter was drafted and sent threatening legal action for the infractions. Within 48 hours, the website had undergone a redesign of sorts with all references to our company products and services removed. I guess that for some people in this world, blatant stealing of intellectual property is the way to success. It didn't matter to the local technology council that she had done this. In fact, they seemed a bit perturbed that I would question her integrity. I was looking to have her expunged from the small community. Little did I realize that I was the one on the outside. A very parochial state where locals formed a close knit bond. Nowhere in their bylaws of council membership was integrity a value to be discussed much less held on high, even for a fledgling information security firm. What should have been in the bylaws was a clause describing the need for genetic ties going back 100 years to ensure entry into the club of the state.

Moving onto Ariel's next incursion into our space. I had been in discussions with a non-profit to provide HIPAA training and support services. All seemed to be going well and a contract on the near horizon was a sure bet. The day came for the meeting to ink the contract. I ventured to my new client's office with final documents in hand about to close the deal. It was not a major deal by any means but another reference account that we would ensure was given more than the value of the contract. Soon after my arrival I was stunned to find out that the contract had in fact been signed with Ariel's company. Under the agreement that Ariel and I had, our training services could be offered through her firm but would need to be taught by my staff using our curriculum which was proprietary. Assessment services were outside her corporate charter or at least that was what I was led to believe. I explained the situation to the head of the non-profit organization and to my dismay found that she was not going to invalidate the contract with Ariel and preferred to go with her regardless of the fact that Ariel had no experience in information security, regulations, compliance or anything remotely close to what was being offered in the contract – the 100 year genetic clause was in effect. I attribute the loss of this contract to the fact that we did not have dedicated sales staff. How else can I rationalize this? Well, my own ineptitude at understanding human nature may be a cause! What is a bit ironic about the whole issue is that the services to be delivered were security and privacy relative to HIPAA. Normally you would think a firm with integrity both in their personal and professional dealings would be the company chosen to deliver services of this type. Even after disclosure to the customer of the issues along with documented proof, the customer still chose to go with those of questionable motives and reputation.

Back to the joint bid for a state contract. The joint bid was a loosely coupled arrangement between three organizations, the third being a regional CPA-based consulting firm. Our company was the lead in the effort engaging Ariel's organization for one area in the contract and the CPA-based firm due to its longevity in the state and name recognition value. Not uncommon in most venues. The bid was for training and assessment services to all state agencies. The content was for basic information security training, IT Service Management training (Service Support), ISO17799 and risk assessment training based directly upon Carnegie Mellon's OCTAVE™[5] methodology. Assessment services would extend beyond the initial training once the training was delivered.

We worked hard to prepare the proposal organizing per state guidelines and per what we perceived to be the key areas of focus. Ariel provided her section complete with misspellings which we re-organized and cleaned up as per any standard proposal process. It was at this time that my partner decided to break the news to Ariel that the final proposal would be submitted without any partner review of the final deliverable. This is standard practice for the prime to not show the full proposal content to the subs on the proposal. Of course this was not taken lightly by Ariel. She believed that we had taken her content out of the proposal as well as any mention of her company. It would have been quid pro

---

[5] OCTAVE® (Operationally Critical Threat, Asset, and Vulnerability Evaluation[SM]) is a suite of tools, techniques, and methods for risk-based information security strategic assessment and planning. See http://www.cert.org/octave/

quo but in fact we did not do this. We just did not want the subs who could be and in fact were, competitors to view the overall tone and content of the proposal. This was a standard case of coopetition and being the prime we had the prerogative not to share our bid information or the pricing. We assured Ariel that all information except for that cleaned up through grammatical editing was left as intended with all company information and backgrounders intact. We were not to be believed and the slander and libelous statements from Ariel about our firm increased tenfold.

As with any government contract, selections are made long after submission. We were not informed that we had in fact won for several months. Once a contract is awarded, the proposal is made public should anyone request a viewing. By that time, Ariel had worked her way into a contracted lead security position for one of the state agencies. It still boggles the mind that someone with absolutely no background in information security could land such a position but it is relative to the organizational awareness of information security in that state at that time and still exists as of this writing as you will see later in this book. It also shows the value of having a sales staff and the ability to sell intellectual vapor.

Over a year after the award was announced we started delivering the services. I contracted with a well-known associate for the ISO17799 training while I would deliver the three other classes. I had just completed all licensing and training for OCTAVE™, which is required by Carnegie Mellon. With the Principles of Information Security and ITSM Service Support classes behind me, I ventured to the statehouse to deliver the final classes. Peering over the class list I noticed entered into the slot for one of the agencies was Ariel's name. After uttering expletives in a few different languages in a continuous string of rhyming epithets, I decided on the following course of action: Classes would not be taught to a competitor who would then use the training against our organization. Knowing that just teaching the OCTAVE™ methodology to an individual does not license them to deliver the course or use the methodology as part of an assessment; I still chose to stand firm since the unscrupulous behavior previously exhibited by Ariel was still fresh in my mind. She would take this course at the expense of the state's taxpayers while being paid by a state agency to attend on their behalf and use this as a step in her efforts to become licensed. Perfect! The next move was a meeting with the CIO.

The CIO was relatively new in the position coming out of procurement and purchasing. He seemed to be sharp enough to take on the complexities and politics of the office as the next few moments would determine. The situation was explained in detail on the relationship we had and the motions filed against Ariel's company. My steadfast position was that the final courses awarded would not under any circumstances be taught to a competitor much less a non-government employee. If need be, he could terminate the contract on the spot and I would go on my way. This was non-negotiable as I was adamant, ready to head to the airport and be done with it. He was not happy but he relented indicating he would inform the agency of the issue offering them an opportunity to replace Ariel with a government employee. I had expected to be sent packing but this battle of wills ended in our favor. It would have been very interesting to be in the meeting when Ariel was informed that her latest plan was foiled. Regardless, it still vexes me that the state would allow a contracted firm to utilize taxpayer dollars to learn a methodology that the offending firm claimed to be expert in and was already offering. This was part of the discussion with the CIO as well. It seemed during the meeting to fall on deaf ears. I would imagine it was standard practice for this state to allow such activity. I was certain that it was standard for this CIO to follow suit. The 100-year genetic clause was again in effect.

During the whole of this process, one of my partners decided to utilize the company name to further his side ventures which were kept hidden to me. Eventually they became evident as his trips to the Washington, DC area were not reported as to the intent, content, or frequency. Meetings with several of his former contacts occurred as he attempted to secure a 'set aside' specifically targeting his side ventures aligned to a certain political party that would also result in a hefty political contribution using a percentage of the set aside as the contribution to that party. This ended when he attempted to have the company pay for his most recent trip. It was time to sever the relationship as ethical bounds had been breached. Maintaining a tie to him would violate the charter of the firm and violate professional decorum as well as erode personal trust to say the least. I hate being seen as a victim and will not tolerate it once discovered. My personality changed like New England spring weather and the one time confidant was severed with immediate effect.

Situational Review

I must take some hits here on several levels as I acted with extreme naiveté in thinking I could trust a competitor with any information regardless of the legal documents between us. Take this as a life lesson. Do not trust a competitor in any form. I should have respectfully agreed to meet with Ariel at her location or a neutral location and let her do the talking – listen first, listen often, listen long. Integrity may be something many strive for and live as an ethos but many others in the industry do not. It is simply a means to an end. CISSP certifications along with CISM should have a background and detailed reference check based upon current and past employment. The cost should be footed by the applicant as a normal course of the process. Standard questions need be asked and answered prior to any granting of the CISSP or CISM titles. There are legal ramifications here that could get ugly but it would weed out some of the undesirables such as Ariel who continues to 'practice' information security today. Much like the kids in school today, everyone gets a trophy.

As for my former partner, I again only need to look at myself for allowing such activity to go this far. When running your own company, surround yourself with people you can trust completely. Anything short of this leads to situations such as those I experienced. You don't need to demand loyalty but integrity is an absolute.

Mangle and Annihilate – The New M&A

The phrase mergers and acquisitions (abbreviated M&A) refers to the aspect of corporate strategy, corporate finance and management dealing with the buying, selling and combining of different companies that can aid, finance, or help a growing company in a given industry grow rapidly without having to create another business entity. Having been through several such transactions in my career, I have come up with a new term for M&A relative to information security and risk, that being Mangle and Annihilate. From here on in this chapter, M&A refers to Mangle and Annihilate. Let's look at the definitions of mangle and annihilate so we are all on the same page.

Mangle - to spoil, injure, or make incoherent especially through ineptitude such as application access *mangled* beyond recognition.

Annihilate - to cause to be of no effect: NULLIFY any controls or: to destroy the substance or force of your information security program or: to regard information security as of no consequence or value or: to cause to cease to exist: as in killing your information security program or strategy or: to destroy a considerable part of information security controls in order to ease the actual merger and/or acquisition.

The M&A experiences I have had border on a new level of illusionary due diligence along the lines of a pro forma exercise so that all boxes are checked indicating that a cursory level of diligence has been taken that is acceptable. Once completed, networks may be joined in a two-way trust whereby those that still care have to deal with the consequences of the pro forma exercise. Most likely, those people have already left the sinking ship. What is desired by those pulling the M&A strings is a zero impact transition relative to security, i.e., a business as usual process. Overnight the risk model of the CISO changes. There are changes in attack vectors, threats, vulnerabilities, impacts, likelihoods of occurrence, levels to which controls are implemented, an increase in disgruntled employees as well as newly opened and extended windows of opportunity for malicious activity. Business drivers and the business itself exert significant pressure to move ahead and sign-off on the pro forma exercises. Who wants to stand in front of the speeding train when their job is already on the line? To do so ensures immediate and swift corporate death and is a suicide by all terms and definitions albeit at the hands of someone else.

Remember all those audit findings you have? Don't forget the vulnerabilities, configuration management issues, patches not deployed, data classification problems and the slew of access issues on your LAN and within your revenue generating applications. Well, once you connect networks, they have just been personified and magnified exponentially. The 'Everyone' group that is applied to multiple directory structures containing sensitive information now allows for the innumerable new employees to add, change and/or delete this info. There is also the unknown and in this case, fear of the unknown which is a healthy paranoia that all information security professionals should hold onto since it is a fact in many M&A activities.

The business is pushing hard to integrate and centralize systems without security in mind; legal is working with outside counsel sending information in the clear via email; employees are downloading, offloading and copying any and all available information while clearing their own information such as email. Data is flowing out of the company and data is being erased on a daily basis. Since it was not highly protected in the first place; since USB drives were not restricted along with CD and DVD burners; since local admin access is allowed; the data flows. As Jeff Goldblum said in Jurassic Park "life will find a way." Data has the same pedigree.

Recommendations can be made to push restrictions using centralized policy management but in many cases I have found that the CIO is not interested in such activity even though the push is transparent for organizations using standard directory services. Requests for increased monitoring vigilance go unheeded. Requests to remove staff immediately upon notification that they are to be terminated are for naught. Risk levels skyrocket but any mention of such is pushed aside as the ravings of the local lunatic, that being the CISO (time for a mirror).

The most glaring situation I have endured is a lesson in how not to proceed with a merger and acquisition effort. It is through this lesson I arrived at the term mangle and annihilate. The M&A effort started as quite a surprise to me having been on board a short few months before the announcement. Like the emotions of death, I quickly cycled through shock, denial, anger and, finally acceptance that the M&A was taking place. I quickly requested a seat on the transition team as an initial requirement ensuring sensitive data was flowing with the proper safeguards deployed and as a longer-term requirement to be at the table during all discussions of layoffs, technology integrations, data migrations, and the like. Something that needs to be in place ensuring the paranoid eyes of the CISO view the activities of transition. I was flatly denied a seat at the table. I continued to press for this access to the point where the requests were no longer acknowledged. What was ironic about this whole process was that the overall corporate lead for risk management denied these requests. He indicated he would cover all aspects of information security and that I did not need to be at the table. What became readily apparent was that he was already positioning himself for a prime slot in the new regime having verbally banished information security and business continuity to an Arctic weather station known as IT infrastructure. One-on-one meetings ceased to occur as did any communication as my boss shunned information security as if we had disgraced our charter. He indicated that he and his staff were working the

106

issues. His staff meaning the operational risk, credit risk, and Basel II staff.

What my boss would discover is that Karma has a Yin and Yang effect to it. The first notification of layoffs (although we cannot call it layoffs but displaced employees) brought to bear the unwanted Karma as my boss and his 'team' were decimated. Within 60 days, 90-95% of his team would be terminated. For the first round, information security and business continuity were left unscathed.

The security group was then relegated to a position of 'status reporting'. We were invited to attend status-reporting meetings on the status reports we would send in on the preceding day so we could verbally status the status report. The status reports we were to status focused exclusively on technology issues and most notably, infrastructure issues and held by a VP one level below the CIO. Being so quickly demoted from a position of information security as a business risk to the archaic view of information security as merely a technology issue albeit infrastructure only forced me to cycle through the emotions of death yet again. From regular meetings with the CFO and biannual board meetings to security as an infrastructure technology issue only. Two steps forward and ten back.

As time passed, we were relegated one level further down the chain as information security was pushed to exclusively a second hand infrastructure issue. This was a move long coming from IT as they desired complete control of the function and most importantly the information flow out of the function. If you can control something you can hide it.

Bad news is not something this organization handled well. As an example, status reporting to the CIO, which in turn flows up the ladder to the CEO and COO, has several colors associated with it none of which is red. There is green, yellow, orange, burnt orange, fuchsia, girlsnberry, hollywood cerise, magenta, maroon, mauve, persian red, pink, pomegranate red, red-violet, rose, rust, puce, sangria, shocking pink, terra cotta, venetian red and vermilion. But no red. Red would mean something is really, really in trouble on all fronts and being a no bad news organization, that could never happen. When I first viewed the report, I was initially amazed at its complexity. A perfect example of reporting through confusion and obfuscation made even more difficult by the 'process for the sake of process' mentality of a member in the CIO's group. It took quite some time to understand the color coding coupled with the left and right arrows, the up and down arrows and what I was seeking and felt a need for, was the left and right slanted arrows and arrows with a larger point size. I was able to find the large point size further into the multiple page report. The report required a legend to the legend to explain all the markings and associated colors. A venetian red left facing arrow could mean several issues existed whereby a green plus sign of large point size indicated everything was hunky dory. I was looking for a sign that would allow me to exit, stage right.

A fantastic case of perception management as the spin doctors worked their magic presenting information in such a way to completely obfuscate the real issues and gloss over the problems that would one day coagulate into a realization that the company must be sold as overloaded systems, ill-conceived development efforts without capacity and performance risk considered, inadequately defined use cases and poorly configured infrastructure led to additional staff in the scores performing manual tasks using spreadsheets to respond to customer requirements as bid in the RFPs. Without significant investment into the multi-millions times ten, the company could not sustain its magnificent growth. Selling the company was the only option. Like a black and white movie from the last century, the boys met behind closed doors at a local hotel working the issues that would lead to massive payouts to the triumvirate of our firm including the cashing in of options, golden parachute bonus (equally up to 3 times their annual salary) payouts along with the fact that they would be kept on for another two years as nearly two thousand employees would be 'displaced.' Greed is alive and well in America only the names have changed (to protect the guilty). Gordon Gekko's "Greed is good" speech was inspired by a similar speech given by Ivan Boesky at the University of California's commencement ceremony in 1986. Boesky was a Wall Street arbitrageur who paid a $100 million penalty to the SEC to settle insider trading charges later that same year. In his speech, Boesky said "Greed is all right, by the way. I want you to know that. I think greed is healthy. You can be greedy and still feel good about yourself." I guess the triumvirate feel quite good about now.

You have to love the terms for firings we have become so endeared with over the years. A prominent example of doublespeak in the corporate world is the number of different phrases that all describe the action of "firing lots of employees", usually obliquely. Like in 1984 we coined the following phrases: layoff, reduction in force (RIF), termination, downsize, rightsize, headcount adjustment reduction in force, realignment, IRIF – An Involuntary Reduction in Force, VRIF - A Voluntary Reduction in Force, eRIF – Layoff notice by email, and WFR - Work Force Reduction. All equal one thing. You are out of a job. Doublespeak is language deliberately constructed to disguise or distort its actual meaning.
Doublespeak may be in the form of bald euphemisms ("displaced employees" for "firing of many employees"). Here are some of my other favorite euphemisms for being canned:

- Sacked, Laid off, Cut, Fired, Downsized, Terminated
- Given the boot, Outplaced, Unassigned
- Let go, Dumped, Uninstalled
- Canned, Cashiered, Separated
- Axed, Shown the door, Made available to industry

- Chainsawed, Bounced out
- Eighty-sixed, Given the old heave-ho, Decruitment
- Reduction in force (RIF), Assignment ended, End of trial period
- Job elimination, Given the package
- We're being forced to negatively amortize surplus personnel
- Some of you will not be going forward with us
- Targeted restructuring
- Aligning the workforce
- We're reconciling per capital productivity with current market conditions
- Refocusing our manpower investments
- Rightsizing headcount to match revenue
- Dynamic rightsizing
- It's like musical chairs … and you don't have a chair
- One person layoff
- Upgrade you with immediate effect
- Let's push the delete button on this relationship
- Synergy related headcount restructuring
- Welcome to Dumpsville. Population: You

The Dilbert comic strip satirizes this in one strip in which an employee understands none of these terms and is unable to figure out that he has been fired. Corporate doublespeak can also involve downplaying problems, such as calling a fix for a software bug a "reliability enhancement." Information security faces the same dilemma.

What is amazing in any time of stress is the fact that true colors of people's personalities manifest themselves. Yes, these can in fact be deemed 'red' in some cases. In this case, people who had kept information security and risk at arm's length overnight became experts in the profession claiming management of scores of systems from a risk perspective and defining information security as merely a policy-generating arm of the now shunned junta once called Risk Management. Survivability reverts the psyche to that of the Id. It was no more apparent than during this M&A activity. Like a puffer fish, résumés became bloated with tasks and objectives once deemed undesirable as embellishment of accomplishments swelled.

The next step in the M&A process was the penetration testing exercise. To be performed by a third party and funded by the soon-to-be new landlords, this exercise I was sure would demonstrate the inherent weaknesses in the people, process, and technology aspects of our information technology environment. The first set of hurdles to jump was placed in our path by our managed service provider. This fine example of technical acumen and highly honed procedural expertise decided to defy the section of the contract dedicated to information security. Short and lacking in content and definition, the section did allow for penetration testing as a normal course of action. During discussions for the M&A pentest, they decided to deny any and all activity as something that would cause our systems to fail.

Something they stated they could not allow due to service level agreements. The fact is that this managed service provider grossly missed multiple service levels every month. The other fact is that as an extension of our IT shop, they were under contract to perform per our design and if we wanted to have a penetration test, we were going to have one (as per the contract). I had recited verbatim during the phone conferences the contract related to information security. Notice as well that our legal department who ratified the contract and IT leadership was also on the calls. Once we stated that the risk is ours, the contract allows for it, and we are going to do this so get behind it, we were able to get over these obstacles.

As the outgoing CISO but still the CISO nonetheless, you would think I would be afforded a copy of the penetration test. Of course I was not. I was told that all copies had to be specifically marked for data classification; number and assigned to an individual for tracking and then destroyed once viewing was completed. In fact, any and all documentation on the fixes had to be destroyed. Below is an excerpt from the contract that really looks like a cover your backsides exercise by the managed service provider:

> Reports and Confidentiality
> Notwithstanding anything in the Information Technology Services Agreement or any related Confidentiality Agreement to the contrary, except as otherwise specifically set forth below, other

than with respect to the report generated by Third Party Consultant in connection with the Assessment which shall remain owned by COMPANY2 and any proprietary and confidential information of COMPANY1 or COMPANY2, any and all information gathered by COMPANY1 or its authorized agents conducting the security testing shall be reported directly to and the property of MANAGED SERVICE PROVIDER and shall be deemed MANAGED SERVICE PROVIDER Confidential and treated in accordance with the Information Technology Services Agreement and any related Confidentiality Agreement. This information, in oral form only, shall only be shared with those at COMPANY1 and its authorized agent, and shall not be disclosed to any other party. This includes a "nothing to report" report. Neither COMPANY1 nor its authorized agent shall maintain any electronic file, e.g. word processing document on VM, PC, removable media, or electronic file containing any information taken or extracted (whether verbatim or in summary fashion) from the information gathered during such testing, including testing results. Additionally, all notes and print outs of any COMPANY1 employee or authorized agent participating in the security test or review process shall be destroyed after the close-out of the final review and shall not be disclosed to any third party.

Notwithstanding the foregoing, the final report (previously approved by MANAGED SERVICE PROVIDER) shall be deemed confidential to both COMPANY1 and MANAGED SERVICE PROVIDER. COMPANY1 agrees not to disclose such final report to any third party except to COMPANY2 and except as specifically required by law, statue or regulation, and then only after COMPANY1 has exerted all reasonable effort to obtain confidentiality protections for such information.

Now I have been involved with multiple penetration tests over the years but never have I seen such a series of legal requirements that completely eliminate all data in any form from existing, after the provider of services approves the report. Needless to say, the report was delivered to COMPANY2; proceeded to go through a series of massages deemed to be 'grammar and spelling' issues that took another week before COMPANY1 (that's us) was allowed to view it. The viewing had to take place at the COMPANY2 location whereby paper copies were distributed and then collected after the viewing (since they had not been classified as yet and no numbers assigned to each and then assigned to an individual). I expressed my displeasure at this as being 'bad form' at the very least. My displeasure had as much authority as a CISO spouting Fear Uncertainty and Doubt (FUD) for the 15th time in 20 days. Hey, wait a minute. I know one of these folks who survived over 5 years doing this. Ah well, later in this book we will discuss this fine specimen of intellectual prowess.

Another meeting was held with the VP of IT to review the massaged findings. The issues could be categorized as configuration and patch management issues. Blocking and tackling that IT and the managed service provider should have learned and accomplished years ago. To me, these issues were complete contract negligence on the part of the managed service provider as the contract specifically stated SLAs for patch management and had specific configuration standards for server operating systems.

The meeting went on without a hitch and the number two man for the VP of IT stated that we would most likely need to execute a request for service (RFS) to get the managed service provider to correct the configuration and patch management issues. I really did not think an RFS was required when contract negligence was at hand. We were allowed to keep the copies at this meeting even though no one signed for the copies of the pentest; none of them were number or assigned to an individual or where they to be tracked. This was obviously a demonstration of effective control by the new landlords.

When going through an M&A, eventually you need to connect your networks. The penetration test was deemed to be the only litmus test for potential security issues. Vulnerability scans, audit issues, identified regulatory problems and other security issues were not to be combined with the pentest and considered as part of the overall criteria in deciding when to connect the networks. The new landlords were not going to get in front of this train. The pentest was completed; box checked; networks connected! All the Everyone groups would now grow in membership. The final pro forma exercise for security was now completed and many thousand investors data, immediately put at risk.

Situational Review

Here are some of a series of tips for security professionals when going through a Merger and Acquisition to help prevent the debacle of the Mangle and Annihilation I experienced:

> Establish an information security transition project team — the role of the information security transition team is that of principal information security and risk oversight for all the information technology, business groups, legal, financial, internal audit and HR groups involved. As such, the information security transition team must function as an integral element of the overall restructuring effort and must coordinate closely with the other teams that will be established for this purpose. The team will be responsible for developing and applying a standard methodology for information security and risk transition as well as overall risk determination.

> Assign a full-time information security transition project manager who will lead and coordinate the information security and risk project from planning through implementation. Members should come from the participating organizations previously established through the business information security officer function or like function, with expertise in key aspects of the

transition effort relative to their departments. In addition, bring in outside third party advisors if required to assist in independent and objective reviews.

Develop the information security and risk transition plan — the plan for information security and risk alignment is a critical component of your company's overall restructuring effort and should complement and easily integrate with the other functional transition plans. The plan should define the step-by-step processes that all business units and the information security and risk team follow and the gaining/divesting organizations must accomplish to restructure information security and risk strategy, program and tactics from a people, process and technology perspective. It should provide an overall concept of operations, describe organizational roles and responsibilities, identify discrete requirements for information security integration when transition systems and applications associated restructuring activities, point out security technical interdependencies, and explain the priority of effort and project schedule as it aligns to the overall timeline for the transition. Of course, dollars are involved and a budget should be created and tracked.

A detailed and extensive due diligence assessment should be executed on the company being acquired. This includes review of all information security and risk functional areas and:

Strategic and Operational practices covering:

Security Awareness, security strategies, goals, and objectives, security regulations, polices, and procedures, policies and procedures for working with third parties, contingency and disaster recovery plans, physical security requirements, personnel security requirements, users' perspective on:

system and network management, system administration tools, monitoring and auditing for physical and information technology security, authentication and authorization, threat, vulnerability & patch management, encryption & identity management, architecture and design, incident management, general staff practices, enforcement, sanctions, and disciplinary actions for security violations, how to properly access sensitive information or work in areas where sensitive information is accessible, termination policies and procedures relative to security, overall data classification efforts, security in the SDLC, application security, security configuration management, security funding, roles and responsibilities within and throughout the company, risk assessment/risk management program, log and audit trail review, event correlation activities, audit findings and internal audit interfaces, regulatory control activities, monitoring program, media sanitization including hardware and software disposal, all policies and procedures (includes information and physical security), investigative and forensic capabilities, vulnerability scanning functions, cryptographic tools, all security technology offerings, listings of all assets, vendor and contract agreements, maintenance renewals and renewal timelines, VoIP review, video conferencing toolsets, mobile device management, etc. The point here is you need to look at everything.

Streamline and accelerate – Where possible, use security as an enabler identifying areas where there is redundancy, communicating standards for information transmission and publishing instructions for how to perform these tasks holding seminars if need be as well as online PowerPoint's, webcasts, podcasts, posters, and handouts non-inclusively.

Staff change will occur. Ensure you are ready for attrition first before layoffs. In most cases, you will lose your most valuable employees first as they are gobbled up in the marketplace. This will leave gaps in your program and likely leave you with you more mediocre employees (as they float to the top). There is definite risk here as performance levels and deliverables can and will suffer. In addition, there will be disgruntled employees on several levels including virtual and physical issues. Workplace violence can occur. Work with HR, IT, legal, and physical security staff to create a transition program for disgruntled employee identification and removal.

Lastly, regardless of their reticence towards including security at the table, force your way to the chair. This is the only way they will consider information security and risk a continued and valuable option. It is one of the most critical times within the organization when threats are high and vulnerabilities exposed. Just make sure you are not identified as disgruntled when getting that chair at the table.

Six Degrees of Deception

What is disturbing about the following situation is that the perpetrator is a CISO. I signed on with this firm since I believed (and still do) that information risk would supersede information security and the risk position would eventually be elevated within this organization, especially since their product sets touted risk as the new savior. I would have to admit that there was significant risk in taking the job since anyone I knew in the marketplace who knew this CISO, knew him to be dictatorial and limited in professional scope. I was not sure what they meant by the last statement but I was sure to quickly find out. Much of my online research on this person, who we will call The Little Corporal, turned up empty. There were a few quotes here and there but no papers, articles, or speaking engagements of any sort. The Little Corporal was not a giant in his industry although as I would soon discover, a legend in his own mind living out inner fantasies evidenced by his fixation on the TV show '24' with his cell and office phone ring mimicking the sounds of the CTU (Counter Terrorism Unit). Nor could I find anything on his educational background which I assumed he would have being the CISO for such a large organization. I also checked with security vendors to find out as much as I could prior to accepting. One such vendor said I would struggle working for this person and that all he knew was technology and even the depth of knowledge there was very limited. Regardless, I pursued this position due to the proximity of my home shunning the other two offers

I had in hand since they were far away. Into the void I strode.

My first tasks were to come up with the top 20 risks impacting the corporation. After nearly 5 years in the role as the CISO, you would have thought these would already be defined and at least in some state of remediation. As I would find, there was a list but it was a hodgepodge of ill-defined issues that were more IT risks than business risks. You could say that IT risks are in fact business risk but for the most part, these were purely technology-focused issues without business considerations. I did my thing defining the top 21 risk issues and delivered the list with potential remediation strategies in a prioritized manner. It landed on relatively deaf ears. Mostly a pro forma exercise since it did not include a theme focused on arresting bad guys. One of the main issues we faced was that of anonymous FTP where many of the corporate customers were listed by folder name just under the top level folder of the Internet facing, completely accessible site. Customers and the company alike would store and forward information in these folders regularly. Sometimes that data was benign other times it was highly sensitive information that clearly violated federal regulations and various statutes. I recommended some very inexpensive options for remediation such as enabling transport layer security within email for point-to-point encryption between corporation and customer making it required as opposed to opportunistic. I recommended open source secure FTP as another option. I was immediately chastised by the Little Corporal for recommending technology solutions since that was not my job; that was the job of the director of information security. Confused that I was not allowed to voice potential remediation strategies of a technology nature, I submitted, providing the findings to the director. Needless to say, the issue was not resolved until a disclosure in the press by a third party well after I left the organization. The response from the organization to the press as a result of the disclosure was to deny any sensitive information existed (even though it was openly disclosed and discussed) and to immediately clean up the site of any and all folders leaving just a high-level FTP site. In checking the site as of this writing (spring 2010), I find that the site is still in operation although it seems that userid / password functions exist on the sub-folders. Regardless, there is no encryption employed. The spice must flow[6].

I later learned that the response by the CISO to this incident was to quickly organize a CYA meeting and directly blaming IT (where the CISO slot reported – the CIO). Openly blaming the CIO is not a healthy act and one that I believe started the process of the CISO's undoing at this organization. I wonder where my recommendations to the CISO and subsequent documentation demonstrating the CISO's and director of information security's decision not to go forward with the Cadillac, Chevy, and Yugo options ended up? I can

---

[6] "The spice must flow." Dune by Frank Herbert Or in non-Dune speak "the show must go on".

tell you they did not see the light of day and most likely reside on some decommissioned hard drive that was supposed to be wiped but now rests in a junk yard in Nigeria.

Over the course of my tenure at this organization it was readily apparent that there was only one way to approach information security and that was the way of the absentee CISO, the Little Corporal. Anytime we tried to apply risk-based approaches to problem solving we were thwarted with the need to deploy new technology. Anytime we tried to employ a comprehensive, holistic approach to technology selection, a deployment that included people and process with business considerations, we were pushed aside like a nuisance child or bothersome secretary. Anytime we wanted to reach out to the business, we were grilled as to our intentions and informed that we could not reach out to anyone higher than our station.

In time, we were able to establish a solid relationship with internal audit (IA). We thought it was solid since I had bimonthly meetings with the senior most IA person in the company. We discussed our risk assessments helping IA define their yearly and quarterly audit targets. I didn't provide all known issues during these meetings, only those related to mission critical systems under some level of development and/or scrutiny. There were many things that I was not ready to deliver until a full discovery and understanding occurred. We (my team and I) spent time reviewing all past audit issues, remediated and open. We examined the projects underway by the CIO. I requested a copy of the CIO's strategic plan but found that none existed. I requested a copy of the CISO's strategic plan but again, a big goose egg. My intent was to understand the directions of the organization so I could focus the risk efforts of my group on what was important. I discovered that the only way to determine this was to attend weekly meetings where new projects were discussed for potential approval or rejection. This too was a bit ad hoc since many times the business was not present to represent their projects. Usually an IT project manager took on this role and most times they did not fully understand the real business intent. When I asked to speak to the business representatives for each business project, I continued to run into the IT project manager. I had to fully explain the need to speak with the business to fully grasp the intent of the system and to define key risk indicators, and still we were prevented from speaking with the business in most cases.

As we began to get by those hurdles and establish some legitimacy within the company, we started sharing our risk assessments with IA. It was a normal occurrence for risk to interface with IA. This started the process of my 'fall from grace' with the CISO. Getting approval to meet with IA regularly required a grilling from the CISO and regular status reports on the events and content of the meeting. I was also able to establish regular meetings with a lawyer within the office of general counsel. In first meetings with both these people I learned of their extreme dislike for the CISO. In fact, they thought he was a used car salesman who was not to be trusted. It was an outpouring of months and even years of anger. They both explained as if on cue during these separate meetings the brow-beatings suffered at the hands of the Little Corporal further describing their inability to get any information from the information security group. The flood of emotion that came from these two represented months and even years of utter frustration at the inability of respected corporate groups to penetrate the shroud of secrecy perpetrated by the Little Corporal. He operated a closed shop communicating only what he wanted, when he wanted to and to whom he wanted. His closed shop was largely a movie set; a façade that when examined closely, any security professional could see it was built on a house of cards ready to collapse at any moment. In my opinion, since the majority of the technologies deployed were signature based, infiltration had already occurred and data was being siphoned off daily. The deployment of a sniffer on steroids technology proved that botnets were rampant within the corporate infrastructure, at least the infrastructure under the auspices of the Little Corporal.

Prior to my arrival, IA corrective action plans were driven directly by the CISO and director of information security. Their methods were combative and uncooperative seeing IA as an enemy and not a partner. My approach was just the opposite understanding that IA has had a seat at the table for years, fully accepted as a corporate partner. The CISO saw them as a deterrent to the program.

As we continued to expand our assessment activities, so too did the discovered audit items. Since we shared our activities with IA, they directed their efforts at problem areas where we were experiencing resistance.

Over the past 4 to 5 years at this organization, the CISO prepared and delivered regular status reports to the CIO, COO, General Counsel, executive board, and the external audit committee. I was asked to prepare a few slides for the CISO for inclusion in these status reports. I did so in the proper business tongue while describing the activities and issues we faced trying very hard to remove any FUD from the message. What I was to learn later is that the CISO would greatly modify these slides watering them down to the point that no new issues were described much less delivered and discussed. He was lying to the executives and outside audit committee members. It is hard to go back and change the message when it has been sung to a specific tune for so long. To do so would admit mistakes. To do so would undermine his stature. Forget stockholder protections. It was all about self-preservation regardless the negative impact to the corporation. Roll the dice and hope.

The risk issues and audit findings started to significantly expand in number and severity. Many of the issues previously identified as resolved were reopened. Many new issues that are truly information security 101 and IT

101 problems jumped to the forefront of IA. Most of these issues could be easily resolved and some were. Some could lead to great embarrassment and unwanted external scrutiny. Many were technology configuration issues but risk was not to solution only deliver the message.

At one meeting called by the CISO when he was not on the road traveling, we started to review the current list of audit items. Before we got into any depth, the CISO uttered a sentence with a word that I had never heard before and one that the spell checker in Word would immediately reject. I can't remember the exact sentence but it went something like this: "the current list of audit items articulateable.'" Confused, I asked him to repeat himself. Once again the word came across the lips of the CISO as if it were truly in the dictionary and used regularly in the halls of the most high. The Little Corporal was at work expanding the English dictionary. It was then that I knew I was finished. I was in the midst of a 'W' having 'misunderestimated' the depths of his overall lack of knowledge. Now I don't see myself as the most educated person but I soon realized that many other new words were appearing on the horizon during these meetings. I wish I could remember them and I imagine that in his new position he continues to reuse the old words while creating new language miscreants.

Over time, I was removed from providing slides for the upper level reports. I learned that the slides were being prepared by the long blue line of loyalists the CISO had surrounding him. They did not consult with me or other risk professionals; they just wrote what they were told to write. Whatever message he wanted was authored by this group. In fact, pretty much any and all communications uttered officially by the CISO originated from this group including submissions to speak at conferences, whitepapers and the like. (I was able to establish strong ties with product groups and even secretly provided the majority of content of a whitepaper that was signed and delivered in the name of the most public facing figure for this corporation.) This contributed to a continued barrage of misleading statements, white lies and well prepared perception management communicated by the CISO up the chain of command. At the same time, IA was delivering a different message, communicating a marked increase in audit items and item severity. Somewhere in the process, IA and the CISO must have collided since the wrath of the Little Corporal came knocking at my door.

The tenure of the CISO was marked by carefully crafted messaging to those above him and a complete gag order on those who worked for him. The cult of personality commanded by the Little Corporal included the loyal minions who I suspect really just wanted to hang onto their jobs. I believe that most acted as his whipping dogs out of fear of termination, not due to a respect for the person.

Technology was purchased and deployed at record rates. This was characterized by bypassing the IT approval process many times, with deployment efforts representing a scant percentage of the technologies features and functions. Very little was documented; roles and responsibilities were not part of the process and security operations received the new technology with little or no training. Most times, security operations had to finish deploying the technology while trying to operate in the existing environment. Most times, the technology was never fully deployed. I would say that at least 95% of the time the technologies deployed were meant to see, detect and arrest. They were not preventative by any means. In fact, they served to fulfill the Little Corporal's need to create a CTU, à la Jack Bauer from 24. The CISO's meetings turned into discussions about bad guys as did the overall security organization meetings led by the Little Corporal. He became obsessed with bad guys. And why not? His whole educational and training background was based upon law enforcement. In the military, working for a civilian federal agency, and being a cop for a small community. His whole being was based upon police work. Bad guys were where he lived. I later learned that he had no formal education outside of high school and a smattering of college courses at a very freshman level. Hard to believe that an organization of this size and stature would hire such a person for such an important and integral role. The Peter Principle in action.

The CISO placed people, some with no experience, in positions of authority based upon their loyalty index. About the only metric used. Neighbors (yes, neighbors within walking distance of the Little Corporal's house) were hired and placed in managerial positions even though they managed no one. The corporate security emergency response vehicle outfitted with the latest satellite phone and other communications equipment was used for hunting trips with his minions. He even drove a shiny black vehicle that mirrored those of state troopers including a built in bullhorn and movable spotlight for the driver side. From time to time, one of his loyalists acted as his driver when he wanted to present an image of self-importance.

Things started to get tense as our disagreements on how to run and manage risk grew. These were not major blowouts or even face-to-face disagreements since he was largely an absentee landlord. When he was onsite, he wreaked havoc believing that the louder one yelled and stomped around, the more people would jump and his many times unreasonable requests would be addressed. IT hated the meetings with him since they were most always targeted attacks against IT.

Since I was not part of the long blue line of law enforcement, I knew my days were numbered. Just prior to going on what would be my final vacation, I had one final low-level confrontation (as most were) with the Little Corporal. Something was afoot with respect to organizational changes and layoffs. Everyone knew it. As an outsider, I was not included in the discussions. My request for information was immediately rebuffed and as I returned from one location to my office, I found the

Little Corporal storming back from the direction of HR. It was at that moment that I knew I needed to present the full package to IA. My bimonthly meeting was the next day and at the end of that day I was off on vacation for a week plus.

I indicated to the senior director of IA my fears based upon my intuition and actions of the Little Corporal. The one-hour meeting lasted over two hours as I described exploitable vulnerabilities, misconceptions on technology deployments, and major risks that were more like major canals, as opposed to minor chinks in the corporate security posture. From major access issues by third parties directly to the core to the now infamous FTP problems (including thousands of internal servers running as FTP servers as well as desktops), I unloaded everything as if on my last couch trip or confessing the sins of the Little Corporal as I received my last rites. Not only did I describe the issues in detail but I provided a roadmap and pointers to prove each issue. The senior director wrote all this down and stated that this was highly explosive information and understanding what to do with it would be difficult. To me it was simple, present the information up the food chain with a plan to validate every item. Go forward and protect the stakeholders and stockholders of the company. I had played the last card in my hand. Off to vacation I went assuming the IA would toe the line and deliver at least part of the message.

Situational Review

As you can imagine, my next day of work after the vacation lasted a scant four hours. IA did not step up. I hired a lawyer to argue the finer points of my package learning after our first meeting that he owned quite a bit of stock in the corporation in question. It was too late to switch at that point since the clock was ticking. He refused to play hardball instead following a muted approach at representing his client.

I would have to say that in hindsight, I should not have taken this position. The outcome was already written. I was thinking of my family first and the position second. I actually thought I could influence people to change their behaviors through demonstrated action. I was grossly wrong. In trying to bring a risk-based approach to the table at an organization marked by a see, detect and arrest mentality, I had failed before starting. It is hard to go back as a CISO once you have built a façade of smoke and mirrors.

You may think that I could have just accepted the role and submitted to the requirements of the Little Corporal but that would have meant falling into the lies and deception exhibited by this group. As you can see, there was no choice. As a CISSP and CISM, and by my upbringing, I had to maintain personal and professional integrity. I owned stock in the company as well and still do. I did not want to see a major breach but then again, I believe it is too late.

I later learned from an outside source the answer to a question that puzzled me for some time. If senior leaders within general legal counsel and IA believed the CISO to be deceptive, how could he maintain his position for so long? The answer came during a chance encounter with a person who knew the story. Apparently (and I repeat this as unsubstantiated, secondary information even though from informed sources), the Little Corporal was running potentially illegal investigations at the behest of one of the corporate founders based upon pure paranoia and conjecture. As long as the information flowed as requested, protections were provided. If true, this would explain many things.

Regardless, the tenure of the Little Corporal would come to an end at this organization prior to moving onto another CISO role as the Peter Principle continues in practice. What is quite funny on one hand yet indicative of the fear perpetrated by the Little Corporal, is that I received several LinkedIn invites from corporate employees I knew well, after he 'resigned' and moved on. With him gone, they could re-establish ties without fear of retribution. One email was marked by the statement, 'the tyrant is gone and anything else will be an improvement.' Direct contact with former staff indicated an overall, joint sigh of relief on the Little Corporal's last day. I only hope that the new CISO, promoted from within the former long blue line starts to realize the need to build a holistic program. Based upon initial reports, I think not since people are comfortable in what they know and at this organization it is technology only. What is an even bigger fallacy is the use of internal security now to sell product informing potential customers of the greatness of their internal deployments. One visitor to this facility, a longtime CISO in the financial services industry contacted me to ask me about what he saw there. A bit hesitant at first, he indicated that what he saw was a highly immature deployment of their technology in such a way that any experience professional could see that it was completely bogus. Even after the departure of the Little Corporal, the deception continues.

I Have Never Not Known Less Than I Don't Know Now

When I first signed on with the mid-sized company where I was the CSO, I promised that I would provide an initial 100-day plan. Within the first week of my new engagement, I did just that (the plan that is). A key item was to deliver an assessment of the overall security posture, something never done before at this firm. The plan was welcomed with open arms by the VP to whom I reported, and by the CIO, his boss. From what I knew about the three previous security officers—the last of whom, I had been told, was fired for incompetence—none of them were up to the task, and I felt confident that I was the man for the job. Fresh off rebuilding a turnaround effort at a much larger and seemingly more bureaucratic organization, I was ready to attack this task with the tenacity of a Zulu tribesman at Rorke's Drift[7].

After a few months on the job and a scant 5 days outside the 100 day window, I delivered a full risk assessment of all information technology (infrastructure and applications) including outbound data flow of sensitive information; physical security at the main campus; gap

---

[7] One hundred and thirty-nine British soldiers successfully defended their garrison against an intense assault by four to five thousand Zulu warriors. The overwhelming Zulu attack on Rorke's Drift came very close to defeating the tiny British garrison, and the British success is held as one of history's finest defenses

analysis; recommended roadmap; costs to become healthy and a timeframe to get there (the financial burdens of which were relatively minimal). Basing my approach on some industry standards—ISO 17799, a NIST standard and Carnegie Mellon's Capability Maturity Model—I put together an integrated risk assessment process that I thought was best suited for the company. Then I set out on my quest to gather any and all information related to the company's organizational and strategic risk. I was determined to examine every anatomical crevice of every device, both physical and virtual. My goal was to get as much information as possible without disturbing the operational environment. The final product would be a complete report of the company's physical and information security posture, along with a prioritized road map of recommended remediation strategies covering people, process and technology.

Unfortunately, I was in for a lot of surprises—not only about a number of serious risks and vulnerabilities at my new employer, but also about the hazards of delivering bad news at another "no bad news" type of organization that would rather affix blame than fix problems.

The first order of business was filling out questionnaires about the security environment, doing vulnerability scans on the operating systems, and conducting a physical walk-through of the facilities. The results were not encouraging. There was no formal approach to patch management, which meant the operating systems were rife with critical vulnerabilities. In addition, the physical environment was so poorly protected that I was able to enter the building after hours, without an ID card or keys, and get physical access to sensitive computer devices in rooms that had been left unlocked. The situation was serious enough that I immediately put together a status update on the security assessment for my manager that included digital pictures of the nighttime adventure. I was also able to gain direct access to the CEO's office. More on this later.

So what else did we discover from a virtual perspective? Let' start with the outbound flow of email. On an average day, over three thousand emails left the corporate boundaries that triggered content filtering notifications. The dictionaries associated with the content filtering were based upon three regulations: Sarbanes Oxley; HIPAA; and GLBA. The email itself and the attachments (Word, Excel, PowerPoint, Adobe .PDF) were scanned searching for keywords, phrases, number combinations relative to these regulations. Items such as:

> Names
> Personal address information
> Dates directly related to an individual, including birth date, admission date, discharge date, date of death
> Telephone numbers
> Fax numbers
> E-mail addresses

Social security numbers
Medical record numbers
Health plan beneficiary numbers
Account numbers / routing codes
Certificate/license numbers
Vehicle identifiers and serial numbers, including license plate numbers
Device identifiers and serial numbers
Biometric identifiers, including finger and voice prints
Drivers license numbers
Credit card numbers
Social Security numbers
Policy numbers
Electronic trading information

- were consistently found and captured as well as legal documents relative to merger and acquisition activities. What was really appalling about the discovery was the overall use of email to send on average over three thousand emails a day that clearly violated multiple federal and state laws. And the recipients were law firms, government agencies in various states, other like firms, banks, insurance companies, partners and individuals. Litigation was argued in email as was the past weekends bachelor party and the filming of unsavory activities. Technical specifications for a new mission critical development effort was being sent back and forth for review and analysis while 'live' data, data using customer information was shared in order to ensure proper system testing. The real clincher here was that some of this data came directly from ChoicePoint a mere 5 months after their landmark disclosures. Whatever you can think of, it was most likely part of the daily email flow as was the merger and acquisition data that being contracts and contract modifications all with Microsoft Word 'track change' turned on so all medications were visible. Great stuff if you want to manipulate stock prices (at a minimum).

The next area of data leakage was relative to the file transfer protocol (FTP). Over three dozen file transfers were found to be conducted on a regular basis whereby userids and passwords were scripted in the clear. Sweeps of our FTP server (by the way, located as an internet facing device within the DMZ) as well as sweeps of recipients FTP servers were tracked and data captured. The findings were disturbing but not unexpected after the email discoveries. Data here included account codes, routing codes, beneficiary data, financial data, policy information, etc. The recipients were well-respected financial institutions, banks for the most part who shared in this regularly occurring breach of confidentiality.

HTTP was the next target area. Much of the data intercepted here related to lost time due to inappropriate surfing of the web. A few employees found it appropriate to buy and sell weapons during business hours ranging from collector's items and AK-47 parts to semi-automatic rifles and 9 millimeter Glocks and Berettas. Other employees found ways around corporate web filtering tools deciding that websites containing sexually explicit material was an effective way to spend their lunch hour. Others searched for high-level jobs at competing firms.

Instant messaging presented another target rich environment. Conversations captured here ranged from invitations for sex to arguments with a spouse at another firm to threats of bodily harm.

My manager was fine with the results but he offered some good suggestions about the most appropriate way to present the information to the CIO. He wanted me to hone the information and more explicitly state the threat of having a given vulnerability. With his suggestions in mind, I revised the preliminary report, removing additional technical jargon and instead relating the threats and vulnerabilities to specific business impacts and regulatory concerns. I tried to put things in simple terms and shrunk the report to only a couple of pages.

I gave the new information to my manager, who approved the content and seemed giddy with excitement about the findings. He said that it was great stuff—that I was finding out what the company's problems were, something they hadn't known before. I felt that he felt that he had in fact hired the right person and he could now take this information for validation of his hiring prowess up the ladder. He gave me permission to deliver an executive summary of the assessment to the CIO in person.

At that point, I was confident in the approach and methods. (Of course I did not include CEO office photos or reference of sitting in his chair in the report). I thought that my manager must be feeling like they had made a good hire, and that he was going to look good by moving this information forward to the CIO. It turned out that what I took for giddiness was in fact the nervous expression of a passive-aggressive personality. He had neither a clue of what was before him, nor any idea of what it meant to our overall security posture no matter how I tried to explain it. This is a man who reminded me of Mr. Magoo. This seemingly kind hearted and gentle man strode through life eyes closed with no awareness of the utter destruction he left in his wake occasionally opening his eyes to look forward capturing a view of the world only to close them again using that view for the next several months as a baseline (much like a point-in-time risk assessment).

I thought of preparing the traditional 27 8x10 color glossy photographs with circles and arrows and a paragraph on the back of each one. Instead, I throttled my enthusiasm to a 10-slide presentation that had my manager's seal of approval. I thought the meeting went extremely well. The CIO asked intuitive questions about how to fix the problems. We talked about patches and configuration issues. Emboldened by the success of this meeting, I headed out to delve deeper into the bowels of the IT organization, moving towards ring zero[8].

More comprehensive application vulnerability scans were next on the docket. The findings about vulnerabilities on the mission-critical applications that drive the business was about to be prepared. Without these applications, the company would cease to exist. Yet these applications were riddled with vulnerabilities. These applications, trusted through standard https port 443 on the firewall, were laced with vulnerabilities that could provide even an ambitious script kiddie with a downhill slide to the company's mother lode of sensitive data. Using vendor provided evaluation software as well as open source tools; we targeted development versions of internet facing mission critical applications. On average, over 800 vulnerabilities related to the Open Web Application Security Project (OWASP – www.owasp.org) Top Ten were found per revenue generation application. Keep in mind that these are trusted applications that have carte blanche access through corporate firewalls. Any breach here, which is relatively easy to do, and it is a downhill run to the mother lode of corporate data. This data was customer information of a highly sensitive nature. And we at one point thought Microsoft was bad? They saw the light and have worked very hard to fix their issues. This firm

---

[8] Ring Zero is a computer protection level with the most privileges and interacts most directly with the physical hardware such as the CPU and memory.

was broken and felt it was okay to limp to the finish line. All any firm needs to do is run scans on their software. It makes nary a difference where the coding is done, US-based or offshore, coders write poor code.

Continuing with the assessment, mission critical application code was found to allow users of the system to see not only their customer's data but other customer's information. Further investigation found that userids were generically established (no named users) and that userids and passwords were hard coded into applications. You have to love it. A final view found that passwords never changed and over 50% were part of the corporate name. Any user upon leaving their employ could still access this mission critical system viewing not only their previous employer's data but the data of others. The data contained personally identifiable information that would seemingly violate state and federal laws. This information was carefully packaged and presented to the CIO and his direct reports. Fast forwarding ahead to present day, this documented vulnerability and the fix for it have yet to be applied as it has been relayed to me through various communication channels.

In following standard ISO17799 framework, I performed a physical penetration test to determine how easy it would be to access the facilities after hours. My assumptions were correct. Access to the building was gained through the parking garage located directly under the main building. Hiding behind a larger air conditioning unit, I waited until a car exited the building.

The garage door remained open for quite some time. Long enough for me and my baseball cap, glasses which I don't wear except for reading, no badge, and a camera swinging on my right wrist to enter. Walking directly to the center of the parking garage, I had an option to take the stairs to each and every floor (as there was no security / proximity card access between floor stairways), or take the elevator again without any security, directly to the executive floor. I chose the easiest pathway to the top. The elevator door opened off the main lobby of the executive suite. No camera at this entrance. Making my way directly through the lobby (directly in front of a camera hidden in the ceiling), I proceeded directly to the CEO's office space. Aligned with portraits of CEOs past, high ceilings and boardrooms with fireplaces, I was unimpeded in my walk to his office. I must say that the CEO's chair was quite comfortable. The expanse of his office enormous. As I sat in his chair I began to think about a day when I too could have such an office working on my laptop going over the financials in front of a roaring fireplace, lights dimmed low, and XM Watercolors emanating over the built-in MP3 system and an admin holding all calls and berating anyone attempting to enter my sanctuary without proper clearance and approval. I'm not sure how long I held this series of dreams but when I came to, I realized that I would never have such an opportunity if I did not complete the task at hand and do so quickly, including getting the heck out of the CEO's chair.

Neatly stacked on his desk was a series of folders and documents, of which the top document was the next day's agenda; timeframes; locations; attendees; phone conferences; lunch meetings; cocktail hour; dinner meetings, etc. Under the agenda were all supporting documents including up-to-date financials, the newest corporate strategies, new hire information and info pertaining to a discussion on the sale of part of the business (a precursor discussion for M&A activity.) A treasure trove of information that I could easily copy on the copier in the admin's area just outside the CEO's office since there was no required copy codes to be entered. I did not notice any cameras in the office area but did not attempt to hide should there be any. For the next two hours I explored the building completely unchecked taking pictures of offices, post-it notes, PDAs, sending email from open PCs (to my own account to prove the access), picking up the full financial package for the quarter prior to public publishing on the printer left there by someone during the day. I was able to access several C-level offices, PCs, laptops, PDAs, personnel files, and more. Other C-level staff left their office doors open providing direct access to PDAs, PCs still connected with no screensavers, personnel files, strategic plans and the latest quarter's financials. Continuing the search to the next floor (while the entire time taking pictures of the adventure) I found a few employees still working. I politely greeted each as I proceeded to enter offices. Laptops with passwords affixed to the right of the keyboard were pretty standard fair. I started to think it must be an enforced policy!

Proceeding to the next series of floors I found row upon row of what looked to be medical records. Records in the manila folders with multi-colored tabs and numbers indicating someone's identity were available in the thousands. Employee cubes were stacked with these as well. Obviously, there was no records management effort to secure, check in/out, and track these sensitive documents. In viewing a few (more snapshots taken) it was found that contents contained medical information, social security numbers, and a multitude of other personally identifiable and private information. HIPAA related documentation on customers was readily available (and still is from what I am told today). I was running out of space on my digital camera. Network closets including the main closet where internal telecommunications termination points were found to be open and direct access to CAT 5 wiring hanging from the ceiling in some cases, made tapping into the network an easy task. I had seen enough. Time to call it a night taking stairs down to the parking garage walking out through the automatic garage doors to my car waiting in the company parking lot.

During the assessment period and immediately after performing vulnerability scans on mission critical application code, I packaged the extent of the assessment at that point. I removed much of the technical jargon relating the threats and vulnerabilities to specific business impact relative to our business and the regulatory environment. I delivered a sampling of the business focused application vulnerability scans to the

CIO with definitions and potential impact. I softened the blow by not providing all the details of the evening's activity. Proud in my efforts knowing I delivered on the promises discussed during the interview process, I stowed the results in secure fashion on the corporate network. I ventured to a security conference possessing the knowledge that the CIO would welcome the discoveries as they served to ensure there were no surprises and that we would be able to organize and prioritize the list of fixes. Again, I resisted the impulse to create 27 8x10 color glossy photographs with circles and arrows. I delivered instead a sampling of application vulnerability scans, describing their potential impact on the business and associated business risks. I did not include photos of the nights escapades instead referenced viewable and easily discoverable issues.

Upon return from a security conference, armed with new information and zest for the job, I noticed a meeting request from the Office of the CIO for first thing Monday morning. My normal paranoia began to take hold but I could not locate a source for the angst although years of professional experience indicated something was not right. I soon found myself in the CIO's office. The CIO had been at this company for several years starting out in true old-fashioned form, coming from finance having zero information technology acumen. Here was a guy who gained the CIO position through the undermining of the former CIO coupled with co-conspirators who still occupied positions within his solidified domain. His main gripe with the former CIO was his cronyism and the kingdom he had built that served to protect and pay homage to the throne.

The door was shut behind me as I entered his office and I was invited to take a seat at the long wooden table. I placed myself directly under the picture of one of the CIO's heroes and proceed to listen to the initial monolog.

The CIO threatened me with termination. The CIO asked me in his very dry deadpan with unanimated features, "Are you committed to this company? This was not the due diligence being sought. Sitting there a bit stunned, I was verbally presented with evidence of my guilt that was being built as a case for termination. It had nothing to do, at least on the surface, with the risk assessment. In fact, the scope of the allegations centered around not responding to an email; not attending an offsite vendor meeting; and not returning from the conference a day early for a meeting called by the CIO at a later date. Of course I denied the allegations indicating I could and would disprove all or provide evidence to the contrary. I was given until that Friday to demonstrate that I was committed to the company. When in fact you don't like the message delivered, then do everything possible to discredit the messenger.

The difference in the delivery and content of the assessment this time was that I was hitting the CIO close to home. If you were to look for the virtual home of the CIO, you would find him nestled within the hills and valleys of these highly complex applications. Standing proudly upon the mountaintop of his layered stack of code, SQL calls and integrated messaging, the CIO was much like the master control program (MCP) in the movie Tron. Months later, I can still hear the words of the MCP echoing in my head: "I can't afford to have an independent program monitoring me."

Emails were collected indicating responses to the email in question. It demonstrated that not only had I responded to the email within 12 minutes of delivery, but I did so on a vacation day copying not only the CIO but several of his direct reports and of course, a CC to myself. I collected airline ticket stubs and weather reports proving that airports had been closed going so far as to secure airline cancellation information on the flights I had changed to get back a day early. Other emails indicating I would not be at the offsite vendor meeting ensuring other security staff would be in attendance were organized for my defense. I carefully organized the evidence so as not to infringe upon the CIOs sensibilities but to ensure clarity without anger. Although I was quite livid at being put in this situation, I started to understand the perception management practices within this firm. Armed with my evidence, I ventured to the CIO's office to layout my case.

We reviewed the data without fanfare and without any apologies of the clearly false accusations. I quickly covered each item indicating dates, times, providing receipts and untainted evidence of my innocence. In the US you are innocent until proven guilty. That is not the case in many corporations where autocratic rule is the norm.

I then proceeded to ask the CIO what the issue really was. Are you trying to get me fired, came his reply?" He proceeded to tell me a story about a former employee who was after his job (as he saw it) and had built a following of staff that did not agree with his policies and direction. Almost like a small internal insurrection that required a swift and violent Soviet style purge.

I found this story to be quite revealing as to the mindset of the CIO. Operating from a defensive posture; from a posture of what I saw to be a feeling of inadequacy in his position; I learned that he had been in the finance group of the firm a short 4 years before and had not been involved in IT to this level. I indicated to him that we would not always see eye-to-eye largely because he was mostly concerned with availability of systems where I was equally concerned with confidentiality, integrity and the availability of systems and data. But my job is and was to keep him duly informed of any and all vulnerabilities and recommended remediation strategies. I tried to explain that I wasn't going after anyone at all— I was just trying to do my job. For instance, when I presented the examples of sensitive information that was leaving the company by unencrypted e-mail, I cleared the names and e-mail addresses of the individuals involved. The point was to show that this type of information was flowing in and out of the company and that there were ways to prevent it.

I told him that while the CIO and CSO are supposed to have some professional tension, in no way was I trying to get him fired. I said that I was trying to let him, as an officer of the company, know where our weaknesses are. I indicated to him that we would in fact have conflicting views largely because he was mostly concerned with developing and deploying revenue-generating applications, where I was equally concerned with generating review for corporate viability, I need to ensure the confidentiality, integrity and the availability of these applications and the data flowing through them. But my job is and was to keep him duly informed of any and all vulnerabilities and to recommend remediation strategies.

Furthermore, I wasn't suggesting that all the code had to be rewritten. There were other things we could do, such as purchase an application vulnerability scanner and give the coders training on writing secure (actually proper) code along with the deployment of application layer deep packet scanning tools (all laid out in the previously delivered report).

The meeting ended with a tenuous understanding but it settled deeply within my psyche that in this company at any time and without reason, charges could be manufactured and staff terminated. The trust factor was gone. I would need to maintain an increased level of vigilance in all matters concerning discovered vulnerabilities. In this company, as in many other such organizations, you are innocent until investigated. Deep down I knew I would never recover from his unfounded attack.

I scheduled a meeting with the CPO (Chief Privacy Officer, an ally in the battle to protect information and one who understands the value of security as an enabler for privacy.) I felt comfortable in my approach and in the knowledge that the CPO would partner with me in this noble quest to protect the assets of the company. The assessment data, clear and concise in its content and intent lie before us on the meeting room table. The CPO, a lawyer by trade had taken this position at the behest of corporate chief legal counsel armed with very little support and a privacy budget of five hundred dollars. Enough as she put it for a couple of dinners with vendors and clients. The CPO position was largely a knee-jerk response to a regulatory requirement and only served to check mark the box on the corporate controls matrix. Several moments of quiet followed by a rising of the CPO's eyebrows led to this pronouncement: "We should take this data and place it under attorney-client privilege," she uttered. Putting this data under attorney-client privilege placed my professional position at great risk. It also was against all the ethical statements signed and adhered to that are part of the CISSP and CISM certification process much less my WASP upbringing. Personal and professional ethics would again be tested. I did not have officers insurance. Nor could I refer to this data should a third party audit our environment. I could not then even use it should we suffer a data breach. As a matter of fact, I would be the target of blame should such a breach occur serving as the proverbial scapegoat being that I was an outsider to the kingdom and the CIO had also worked to discredit the messenger who brought this data to the table that was not being earmarked for double secret classifications and deep sixing. It would be determined that I had not performed my duties as defined and required. As an employee of the company I would be legally bound by this covenant not able to speak of it; to reference it; to use it to support the remediation strategies currently outlined in the prioritized roadmap. I would be the whipping boy for the failures of corporate officers to act according to the trust bestowed upon them. I voiced all the above and the matter was dropped. It might have been due to the frothing about the corners of my mouth that got their attention. I'm not sure. For the current round, since fights of these types tend to rear their ugly head at the most inopportune times, I had won a small skirmish.

What I found and continue to find in my interactions with CPO's who are lawyers is their inability to think without the ever present legal mind that serves in some privacy matters to cloud the situation. It is not always a legal issue. Ethics must play a role. Chief legal counsel and his/her office exists to protect the company and within this vein of thought, self assessment data not being under the guise of Internal Audit could be hidden and obfuscated. This demonstrated and continues to do so at other organizations the overall immaturity of information security, privacy and compliance within corporations. Even though information security may have a seat at the table at some companies, the function is still not fully inculcated into the fabric of corporate governance in such a way that ensures integrity at all levels. Going back to the ethos that information security professionals must and do follow, this places a natural, daily strain on the position and overall functional information security organization.

Soon thereafter, my reporting structure changed. The security function would now report to a different VP within the CIO's office, that being the CTO. Possessing the optimism of new management, I started to communicate the risks as documented and those under review. These were done in person and through email. My use of email was a normal course of action but became a method for tracking and validation especially since the latest interlude with the CIO. I made of point of following up our face-to-face meetings with email recaps of the meeting and decision points. I carbon copied myself and applied read receipts to each email. The emails and read receipts were stored and archived. Of note, the VP informed me under no uncertain terms that continued communication of these risks via email would not be healthy for my career. His reasoning was not due to the content but due to the sheer number he received on a daily basis. I indicated that I need to ensure proper follow-up and tracking of our discussions to ensure tasks were addressed, goals met and information clearly understood. He relented a bit but continued to voice his displeasure and communicate the threat.

After full review of all gather information, roadmaps, assessment info with my new boss, a much smaller package was prepared for the enterprise risk committee. After several reviews with the VP, CIO and other leaders outside the technology department including the VP of Internal Audit (who in fact sponsored the meeting with the risk committee seeing that he was in fact the chair), we were ready for the presentation. It went swimmingly with just the right amount of astonishment at the findings and confidence that they had the right person in place. The FUD for FUNDING presentation hit home (warning – use sparingly). At one point during the meeting, a high-ranking attendee recommended we centralize the security, privacy and compliance efforts and that I should lead the effort. Utter glee does not adequately describe the emotions flowing through me at that time. The next meeting was set. Onto the boardroom!

A new presentation made its way through the obstacle course of reviews and modifications. Discussions and changes. Changes and discussions; Meetings to discuss meetings about new meetings to be held and what to discuss in those meetings were held. Once all had reviewed the document within IT including the CTO and CIO, providing their blessing with the final product (this took about six weeks), I hand delivered read-ahead materials days in advance to the administrators of the corporate leadership. The morning of the day came. Anticipation was high. I felt butterflies in my stomach of which I had not experience in several years. It was the feeling I used to get before a big game. Palms sweating, stomach in knots, but an overall good feeling that I knew upon the first words uttered from my mouth would subside and the information would flow. All was set. Documentation prepared. Backup laptop in tow. I made my way about 30 minutes ahead of time to the CEO's private conference room. Upon entering the room I was intercepted by the CEO's administrative assistant. Although the greeting was pleasant the message was not. The CFO had called indicating the meeting was off. My heart sank and my mind started to race again much like it had prior to the fateful meeting with the CIO. I made my way back to my office to find an email and voicemail from the VP of Internal Audit indicating the meeting was cancelled. On the heels of the first call came another. The meeting was on but only with the CTO, CIO, CFO, the VP of Internal Audit and me. Immediate disappointment turned to renewed but tempered excitement.

I sat at one end of the table in a conference room with a view of a hilltop golf course. To my right were the CTO and CIO. To my left was the VP of Internal Audit. They were not next to me but at the far end of the conference room table. Soon the CFO walked through the door. The PowerPoint covering the details of the read ahead was ready on the screen. Corresponding printed copies in front of each attendee.

"Shut that damn thing off. I don't do PowerPoint's! Didn't anyone tell you, said the CFO?" Through all the meetings, discussions, and hashing over of the details as

159

well as sitting there setting up the projector, no one had decided to give me that small detail. Know your professor, get an A. I was starting off already with a hook.

The CFO cut right to the chase. "How the hell did you get this information," he snarled holding up the pages on the merger and acquisition information. In what must have been no more than a nanosecond but what seem like quite the duration held in suspended animation, I drifted off to the days of lie detectors and harsh questions during the espionage interviews we had to go through just to gain entry back in the US. Although the Office of Special Investigations (OSI) staff delivering the questions and testing were "friendlies," (yes Steve Austin there is really an OSI), their methods were not about mom and apple pie. I was immediately placed in a defensive posture. Sitting alone like a pariah at one end of the table, four sets of eyes were upon me. One set was in my camp but the other three were definitely not friendly. If emitting an 'identify friend or foe' signal at that time I would have prepared for immediate hostilities.

I tried to explain that we used a sniffer much like an eaves dropping device to identify information flowing out of our infrastructure based upon keywords and phrases and this information was part of the haul. After a few snide remarks to the effect of 'what did we hire a 007' as an attempt on his part at humor, the CFO proceeded to drill down on this issue. Right away I had lost any semblance of control of the meeting. To think you will have control of a meeting with C-level staff is ludicrous at best but communicating an agenda and attempting to follow is a must regardless of the direction they take you. Questions along the lines of 'who has seen this' and 'do you know that only 10 people in the company are supposed to know about this and I gave very clear instructions that anyone divulging this would be terminated on the spot' were peppered with a reversion back to the initial question of how did I get this again. It was also clear that the CFO wanted to know who was sending this information out via email without securing it. Informing him that it came from legal gave him a chuckle. "Does chief legal counsel know about this," he smiled. Certainly as we had communicated this to the chief privacy officer sometime ago. "Well why don't they protect this type of information," he pondered openly. Same question I had, how about that!

A series of solutions for securing outbound email had been prepared and documented. We had researched a solution and the CIO and his lengthy chain of command had all approved the purchase of the hardware and software. A mere seventy thousand dollars and we could mitigate the outbound data flow of sensitive email. We could be seen in the industry as a leader in the quest to maintain the privacy of our customers. I saw this as a marketing opportunity to further define our position while those around us suffered data exposures and breaches of various types. The CFO agreed and asked when the solution could be operational. In a fit of optimism, I indicated it would take two to three months but definitely before year's end. It was currently early September. It was a small victory but one nonetheless that I would gladly take. Other questions flew and flashbacks to previous days of like interrogation circled in my head like wagons on the prairie. A suggestion was made to place posters around the building with my picture as the adorning attraction, serving as a warning to those who saw me to cease-and-desist any activity contrary to the principles of security and privacy. At one point, I vowed to myself that I would place a in the CFO's office on my last day but my senses came to me when that day did in fact arrive. The poster incident was another turning point where I knew that any efforts to perform my job to the degree required were for naught. Even at the CFO level, this was nothing more than a mere irritant. Regardless, armed with the knowledge that we had won a battle, I left the meeting with a confused feeling of both triumph and resignation.

So why do you think the original meeting was cancelled? Let's follow the organizational trail here to see where the buck stops with respect to ownership. I report to the CTO who reports to the CIO who reports to the CFO who reports to the CEO. If there are issues in the IT environment relative to data leakage as was demonstrated, then the CFO is in fact responsible. For that matter, all corporate officers are responsible. Regardless, the CFO had finally read the read-ahead that morning and realized the magnitude of the FUD and decided to shutdown any discussion with his peers. His peers in this case were the COO, CEO, Chief Legal

Counsel, and others. He was not prepared for the meeting since he had not read the information provided. Nor had he been adequately prepared by his direct reports on the content and tone. He decided to manage the perceptions of those above him by restricting access to the source and downplaying the issues in the document. Most likely no one even read it at that level even though I hand carried it to their offices. What I also should have done was insisted upon a signoff sheet for receipt of a controlled document and then followed up with an email to the corporate risk committee indicating that the document had been delivered and was available for their review. .

Within one month of this meeting, the climate began to change. At least that was my perception. The CIO now wanted to know who else in our specific vertical was using such a tool. How were they using it and what did the customers think of the use. Was it easy to use? Now understand how difficult it is for security professionals to find this information out specifically on what your competitors are doing and you will understand the intent of the CIO. I believe he sincerely wanted to know what the competitors were doing in this space but that to me was irrelevant based upon the level of risk associated with the flow of sensitive information outbound from the company. Regardless, it gave a view into the mindset of the C-level staff. If our competitors were doing it then we must. If they are not, then why bother.

After continued lengthy discussions with the CIO on the uses of the tool (which by the way was provided in a document attached to the PO embedded in the purchasing system as required by policy) now fully understood that the solution would require many recipients of the email to click a link and enter a password to get to the now secure email. This was not acceptable. Having to perform 9 to 10 additional keystrokes was not seen as 'ease of use' for our business partners. The risk of having them tire from the onslaught of additional keystrokes far outweighed risk of data leakage that could lead to a corporate reputation issue, a drop in our bond rating or stock price and a subsequent legal investigation at the least. It outweighed the fact that the people who would tire from these additional labor-intensive keystrokes could in fact be the ones whose information was being disclosed. I attempted to partner with marketing staff on the value proposition that such a tool would offer and the way they could weave this into their messaging. They were not impressed and would not even consider this a viable option.

I quickly queried our vendor partners as to who in our specific vertical were using such a tool. Combined with Gartner and Forrester research data and some support from the VP of Internal Audit, I was able to find five companies using such a tool. There are of course dozens of others but the request was for our specific vertical. In thinking about this request, I felt I had been reduced to irrelevancy. What reason could it make if one or ten such companies use the tool or even none? The regulatory and statutory requirements were clear. I drifted to the courtroom and found myself standing before a white haired judge having just pledged to God that I would tell the truth and nothing but the truth. A stern-faced prosecutor approached and asked the question that in my dream I found I was more than ready to answer: "Why didn't you deploy the solution that the CIO, the VP, Enterprise IT, the VP of IT Finance and the CFO had all approved for purchase?" Confident and smug in my response, I loudly retorted: "Well sir, no one else was doing it so we felt we didn't have to either!" Once the words, syllable by syllable, emerged from my lips, I realized how incredibly foolish this sounded. I pictured lemmings jumping to their deaths off a tall cliff with jagged rocks and rough seas below, me smack dab in the middle. My lawyer had guided me that this defense, much like a liar-liar pants on fire defense would work like a charm. As I drifted back to the pseudo reality that lay before me, I grew angry that I had been duped into wasting time to find out what other 'like' companies were using as a solution. Regardless, like a good soldier I presented the findings only this time in the form of an overall risk finding. Something we like to call a BARF (Business Acceptance of Risk Form) or a risk letter.

The name is apropos since we are ensuring that the ugliness of the risk is clearly transferred to those who choose to ignore the layers of safeguards and protection strategies provided to them during the overall process, and then to accept it. The BARF makes certain they are aware in writing of our trusted advice and options to remediate.

Since electronically sending this document to the VP of Enterprise IT there had been but one comment that being verbally: The companies I had identified were in fact in our specific vertical but there is an even more specific, specific vertical. Since the five firms I found were not in the specific, specific vertical, we would not be deploying the solution. What I mean by this is that even though the firms identified fit the description of 'competitor' there was another level of definition of 'competitor' I had missed. This was something akin to 'really, really close competitor.' I asked who these companies were and I never received an answer, which in itself was the answer. Feeling like it was some sort of double-secret probation and I was about to get a zero point zero GPA, I left that meeting knowing that this document would never be signed. *(Double-secret probation is a condition of arbitrarily imposed scrutiny of a given person's or group's activities in an organizational or academic setting without procedural warning.* But, I did in fact track the sending of the email with this document attached and captured the read receipt that demonstrates the email had been opened. I had delivered a document approved by the CIO in form and procedure, only this time it was to the CIO and his direct report (both officers of the company). The verdict is still out on this particular subject and has not been deployed as of this writing. I could go on with more stories of ethically questionable activities directly attributed to this company, but I believe the point has been made. The vortex swirls around me as I stand on the precipice of integrity looking into the void of unethical behavior, wondering when the next meeting with the CIO will occur. How can I stay and live up to the Code of Ethics or the Corporate Code of Conduct? How long can I continue to present the risks and hope to survive? I did what I was supposed to in my position that being presenting the risk weighed against the threats and vulnerabilities, likelihood of occurrence and overall impact of the business risk after viewing existing controls and degree to which they were applied and working. I offered multiple safeguard options and various protection strategies incorporating people, process and technology including cost benefit analysis and value propositions. What more could they ask for? Some may say that I need to remember who is providing my paycheck. I do remember but to look the other way or to openly condone the lack of due care and diligence would betray the profession. What do I do with the breaches discovered this day on another mission critical system, especially when initial investigation demonstrates VP and CIO awareness for several months? Where does my career go from here if I break under the weight of their considerable pressure? Should whistle blowing be an option? Would you say that based upon a standard Code of Conduct that there were various levels of retaliation that could have been used against me? What potential violations of this code occurred in the scenarios describe in this chapter?

To cap off this chapter, it is amusing to know that after leaving this firm the security team received national recognition for their activities as a team. I'd like to take some credit for this as I was the CSO at the time and did suggest the submission for the honor and wrote the recommendation for the team. In spite of all the negative pressure from the CIO and others within, the team was able to execute to the strategic plan while removing nearly $250k in hard dollars from the annual maintenance expense budget for information security while at the same time expanding and enhancing the overall security posture. This team is one of the finest groups I have ever worked with and would welcome the opportunity to do so again. Under intense pressure we were able to execute to a high degree creating a 'World Class' security team while swimming in shark infested and polluted waters. In closing, I must say that the internal posting on the corporate intranet at this firm as an announcement of this award was submitted by the CTO of the firm without the team's knowledge and directly attributed the overall IT organization as the recipient of the award and not the security team itself indicating as well that the company takes security very seriously and as a result is of very high value to the customers. The overall message from the CTO continues to reinforce the message that was the theme of this chapter and the whole book. The illusion continues as per the actual sanitized intranet below:

News & Communications

IT Named "Best Security Team" by Industry Magazine

Magazine, in its 2007 awards edition, has named Company IT "Best Security Team." ....the Awards program honors the best and brightest security professionals, organizations, vendors and service providers.

Company IT was recognized for its successful efforts to strengthen training and expertise around information security, privacy awareness, risk assessment, auditing, and identity management. Current CSO name, The Company's chief security officer, represented the company at the awards event.

Other finalists in the category included 'Large Financial Services Firm' Information Risk Management Team, and the 'Federal Agency' Office of Computer Security.

"Information security is critically important to our company and our industry. So we are especially pleased to receive this award as acknowledgment of the commitment and focus of so many talented people in our organization," said name, chief technology officer.

"Our partners and customers can have confidence that information security is a top priority for our entire organization."

Prior to leaving this organization the security budget for the coming year was cut by over 57%. That amount was cut by another 10% before I left. After I left, the remaining paltry sum was cut again another 50% leaving my former team and the new CSO with just enough money to pay for an internal project manager for a few months and a couple of small capex purchases. The email issue remains. All from the firm that sees information security as a top priority.

Situational Review

Communicating with the C's

You've spent the past few months collecting information, discovering vulnerabilities and determining gaps in your physical and information security environment. It's like a full physical examination, including upper and lower GI series, blood tests, MRI and prostate check. Prior to this effort, the corporate executives found ignoring security issues to be a cost effective method of risk management, largely because you could provide no hard data on the losses they face. If you can't identify breaches or attempted break-ins, the board has no incentive to buy safeguards, execute the protection strategies and organize properly to combat threats. But now it seems the stars are aligning to facilitate a security breakthrough. Your "exam" identifies threats and assesses vulnerabilities for the potential loss, modification, disclosure and destruction of mission-critical information; the results show where the attacks are coming from, their frequency and intensity. Meanwhile, record numbers of breach disclosures flood the media. States are pumping out new privacy legislation with amazing regularity that further establishes awareness for the cause. The time approaches for funding priorities for the next fiscal year. Surely security will be properly funded for the first time in corporate history?

Wrong! Regardless of what the data says, if you do not communicate in a way that speaks to the sensibilities of the corporate C's without political embarrassment, they won't get the message. So how can you craft the message in such a way that you can be sure it will penetrate to the appropriate level?

Below are some communication strategies I learned, applied and could have applied better:

1. Seek out a trusted sponsor—a person who can serve as a conduit to getting your message heard. I found the VP of Internal Audit to be a great ally. Internal Audit (IA) has been trying for years to get companies to comply with their findings; they follow a code like you and I. Your efforts will only help their cause and they in turn can assist you in driving home the need for proper safeguards and protection strategies. Align your information security pitch with their internal controls–oriented message, adding specifics relevant to the 10 domains of ISO17799 or CISSP Common Body of Knowledge. Deliver the security risks as business risks communicating directly to IA any/all issues relative to the regulations and statutory rules. Document within the risk assessment process that all RAs make their way to IA including any and all BARFs. I guarantee you that most CIO's and CTO's will not like the process and may even try to suppress the flow. Remember, as the head of security, you are charged with safeguarding the assets of your company. It is imperative that you do not rest and you persevere through what will become very intense pressure.

2. Make sure the emperor does have clothes. Communicate proper issue awareness to the CIO on more than one occasion prior to the board-level presentation. Do not lie. Ensure your message is both accurate and true. There is in fact a difference. Accompany this message with details of how previous investments have led to measurable wins. Articulate in the proper level of detail the business risks at hand. Deliver the bad news as required. It is your job to ensure the CIO knows. Do not hide information regardless the magnitude of the risk. It is just such risk that must be communicated.

3. Have a clear plan in hand. Articulate a well-defined two-year time line for risk remediation and optimization. Include funding requirements with capital amortized and resources defined at least at a rough level. Present the plan as both a strategic plan and a prioritized roadmap that needs CIO input for validation. Ensure the CIO knows the priorities may and most likely will change as other risks are discovered and current risks are remediated. Clearly define the key performance indicators and critical success factors for the plan. Ask the CIO for their buy-in and concurrence. A critical success factor is the CIO's understanding of the plan; buy-in to the plan; and communication to other business leaders for the need of such a plan.

4. Know your professor; get an A. Query those who have had at least one audience with the C's as to their style and expectations. Learn of their personality types if possible (the Myers-Briggs test is one good way to approach this task). Most technology types are ISTJs (Introverted, Sensing, Thinking, Judging) according to the Myers-Briggs Type Indicator. They are introverted by nature and varying degrees. Sensing, thinking and judgmental. They are detail oriented and require such detail in order to make decisions. You'll find that without the proper level of detail, your initiative stalls. Make it a point to explore personality types. If need be, directly ask the CIO and his direct reports their type indicators. You need to understand the hot buttons not to push and those you must push in order to succeed.

5. A good idea before its time is not a good idea. Examine the current corporate climate for proper timing. Make sure that there is no current crisis that will preoccupy the executives' attention during the delivery. Nevertheless, don't wait too long regardless of the timing or the window of opportunity will pass. Many ideas fail not because of their merits but due to poor timing. A good idea is good if you can make it their idea. This is an art form and mastery that includes an understanding of the personality type described in number four above. This is not manipulation but a business method. Great ideas come and go daily. Leaders love to look good. Plant the seed fertilizing it to grow over time.

6. Surprises are great for birthdays but not for board meetings. Communicate to the leadership team that a read-ahead is coming. Provide it at least three to five days prior to the meeting. Make it clear and concise. Your trusted ally will help you determine what is acceptable in your environment. Hand-deliver and gain admin sign-off of receipt. A properly vetted read-ahead and presentation makes for a smoother meeting. Executives do not like to be blindsided and looked the fool. Ensure they do not. At the start of the meeting, give it one more review of the read-ahead asking if there are any questions prior to moving the meeting along.

7. Test the waters. Deliver the message to a risk committee or other such group. Ask for immediate feedback on the effectiveness of the message. If they do not get the message, you can be sure the Executives will not either. Ask them pointed questions on whether the COO will be receptive to the message. Query them on both the content and the style of the presentation. It may be that the Executives never use an LCD projector and PowerPoint. They may very well expect all meetings to be paper driven. Do not make this mistake. As the questions necessary on content, flow, style, and delivery mechanism and type (paper - overhead - PowerPoint).

8. Know your company's industry. Like a professor about to teach a class, know everything about your industry, including all surrounding environmental activities and trends within your vertical. Be prepared to discuss what your competitors are doing regardless the relevance.   Deliver   the   message   as   a   market differentiator.

9. We are not alone. Ensure the C's know that this is a journey and that they are not alone in their efforts to provide proper protection strategies and safeguards over their mission-critical data. Let them know that the risk is universal but we cannot afford to have a public embarrassment such as many before us. The risk is not information security risk but corporate risk and should be aligned with all other such risk in the company and weighed in comparison to these. Funding should be provided based upon these weightings. Using FUD for Funding is okay but don't cry wolf.

10. Be confident. If you have followed these steps, you have reached the top with a well-honed message, regardless of the outcome. There is not more you can do short of standing on the table jumping up and down screaming and yelling. Of course this won't work and you will be escorted out of the building. Maintain a log of all transactions in communication.

If you are in the wrong organization, it is a good idea to get out on your own. If you cannot, then you may have to follow some of the following words of advice. I know I said above that if you know your professor you will get an A. But A may also stand for something else. A is for Attorney. If you face termination due to doing your job with the utmost integrity then secure an employment lawyer. Just make sure they don't hold stock in the target company. This will cloud their judgment. When the time comes, negotiate your package by striking unreasonable language. There will be plenty of it. Make sure you tell the truth at all times but mostly after the check clears and all legal documents are in place. You may also wish to rent a safe deposit box. If so, do it under your spouse's name. Document all your conversations, back them up and place them in the safe deposit box. This is the only time as a security professional you use insurance for security. Once you have placed all this information in the safe deposit box, turn in your CISSP and CISM since you have violated their codes of conduct and ethics. You have become one of them.

Paranoid? A bit. With reason? Absolutely. In the immortal words of Alfred E. Newman: "What, me worry?"

Illusion of Due Diligence

Throughout this writing we have spoken of the types of activities information security professionals engage in, in order to comply with federal regulations and statutory laws. We have also discussed corporate governance including IT governance as models used to ensure proper due diligence is executed as part of corporate efforts to comply with these regulations. Many organizations and I may even venture to say most actually have the best interests of the stockholders and employees in mind. However, there are other corporations who intentionally build walls of bureaucracy and insurmountable hurdles that prevent full due diligence to occur. A recent example outside of those already discussed concerns a recent reorganization of one firms internal audit functions.

The internal audit I knew while at this company was one that wanted very much to maintain the integrity for which they were known. The VP over this organization lived the definition of the word. His military background demanded it. His own personal mores ensured it. This VP exposed technical and procedural inequities in compliance, information security and of course audit all while working within the processes and procedures of the firm as established through their governance programs. It was always a pleasure to interface with him. Once he left, the interim leadership initially continued on with his agenda but as time went by, the zeal and drive to continue to carry the mantel of what he stood for faded.

Soon a new VP was hired from one of the Big 4 accounting firms having been a senior manager providing outside audit review of corporations like this one. Prior to his current tenure, the organization had an open door policy where information flowed from top to bottom to top without fear. Emails, phone calls, walk-in meetings all occurred as a normal flow of operations. The new organization now in place gives pause on several levels.

Currently only direct reports to the new VP are allowed direct communication to him. Now emails are to be sent directly to him. No phone calls are to be place directly to him. Now letters or internal correspondence is allowed to flow directly to him unless it goes to his direct reports first. All avenues of communication must follow hierarchical protocols ensuring multiple layers of filtering. It begs to ask why would an internal audit organization built to ensure compliance and weed out issues that can bring about significant unwanted attention to corporate officers establish such protocols. How can anyone low in the internal audit organization ever be sure that the message as intended and as written ever makes it to the top? What purpose does such an organizational structure for reporting serve? Is it in place to ensure no accountability? How can there be accountability within such a structure unless a technical popcorn trail is established with each keystroke? How would someone think to create such an organization in such a way especially when the architect of this structure came from a Big 4 firm where accountability is required? Does this smack of accounting scandals of the past? Why is it that several former employees of this Big 4 firm now work in leadership positions at that firm in question? Remember Enron? Let's refresh our memories here. According to Ms. Sarbox (Sarbox, 2003):

> *"Once upon a time in a great, great land, she says, there was a company called Enron. It did not live happily ever after. This made the people of this great land confused. "What is happening?" they cried. Tell us, oh great Arthur Anderson! I cannot, was the reply, and the people were stunned. Soon other companies began to not live happily ever after, also, and the people grew ever more confused. They began to suspect that some of the officers of the great land's public corporations were not always completely truthful.*
>
> *Then the people of this land discovered that it was not actually against the law to be untruthful sometimes, and there was a great outcry. Fix this! They beseeched their elected leaders. Pass a law! And so the great leaders of this great, great land did."*

Another fun fact to keep in mind is that according to a survey conducted by Starwood Hotels and Resorts (Ethics Roll Call, The Institute for Law Enforcement Administration, 2002):

- 99% Consider themselves honest in business.
- 87% Have golfed with someone who cheats.
- 82% Personally cheat at golf.
- 82% Hate others who cheat at golf.
- 72% Believe golf and business are correlated.
- 67% Say a golf-cheat would also cheat at business.

How many of the remaining 18% are lying? If they cheat there, where else do they cheat? Is it really that important to falsely lower your score? If 82% of them cheat, how can 99% of them call themselves honest? Are you really that insecure?

One would ask the question of this new VP of Internal Audit who worked with the likes of David Duncan at Arthur Andersen. Let's take a look at the scandals from a high level (not in any particular order):

Bernard Ebbers – WorldCom - $191 Billion in shareholder losses
Ken Lay – Enron - $68 Billion in shareholder losses
Sam Waksal – ImClone - $5 Billion in shareholder losses
Dennis Kozlowski – Tyco - $100 Billion in shareholder losses
John Rigas – Adelphia - $15 Billion in shareholder losses
David Duncan – Arthur Andersen – Not a public company
Dick Cheney – Halliburton - $22 Billion in shareholder losses

George Bush – Harken - $850 Million in shareholder losses

Joseph Naccio – Qwest - $108 Billion in shareholder losses

Gary Winnick – Global Crossing - $47 Billion in shareholder losses

Now I am not saying that this is occurring at this firm nor am I implicating the new VP of any such activity. What I am intimating is that activities of the sort in the top ten above have to start somewhere. They start small and grow. Management will take queues from those above them on what is or isn't appropriate. They will emulate the personalities of those above them and in most cases follow the guidance given them from their superiors.

I have taken the issue of the organizational structure put in place by the new VP out to left field and into the bleacher seats but why not ask the questions and ponder what rummages around the synapses? If no one is allowed any direct communication to the top except through the imposed hierarchical structure, how can internal audit due diligence be assured? Add to this the fact that internal audit activities at this company that focus on information technology have dropped off since the advent of the new VP and one must begin to wonder. Is there truly due diligence or just the illusion of such? If all the boxes are checked and signatures are applied, then diligence must have taken place. The question of how far down to dig comes to mind. If I dig down one foot I will find manageable issues. I will resolve them;

document the resolution; communicate this and gain accolades and deliver the report covering the one-foot excavation as meeting any and all corporate governance requirements. What pray tell would happen if someone decided to fully excavate the site? If you know there is gasoline contamination in the soil, do you dig down one foot or do you keep digging until all contamination is identified and at the very least, plans put in place to clean up the contamination? Keep in mind that as you dig through the contaminated corporate soil that your job may be on the line. As a security professional, I see my charter as that of full excavation. Corporations don't want you to dig beyond prescribed levels. It is even hazardous today to discover code vulnerabilities associated with websites and then to communicate these vulnerabilities. The web makes creating software vulnerabilities easier, disclosing them more difficult and discovering them possibly illegal. Why would discovering them become illegal? What is the reasoning behind such thought patterns? I can attest to being threatened with termination when I started to expose vulnerabilities in the code of mission critical applications at the same firm that now employs the new VP of Internal Audit. I dug too deep threatening to destroy the canopy of false coding excellence perpetrated by the CIO and his minions as part of their perception management program repeatedly documented as CMM Level 3 (which actually was a measurement for one application from 3 years past). Let's take the case of Michael Lynn formerly of ISS (now IBM) who found a critical vulnerability in the IOS of Cisco routers.

While at a Black Hat conference in Las Vegas, Michael Lynn, a former ISS researcher, and the Black Hat organizers agreed to a permanent injunction barring them from further discussing the presentation Lynn gave on Wednesday. The presentation showed how attackers could take over Cisco routers; a problem that Lynn said could bring the Internet to its knees. The injunction required Lynn to return any materials and disassembled code related to Cisco, according to a copy of the injunction, which was filed in US District Court for the District of Northern California. The injunction was agreed on by attorneys for Lynn, Black Hat, ISS and Cisco. Lynn was forbidden to make any further presentations at the Black Hat event. Additionally, Lynn and Black Hat agreed never to disseminate a video made of Lynn's presentation and to deliver to Cisco any video recording made of Lynn."

Another such instance involved the well-respected Dr. Pascal Meunier of Purdue University as reported in his blog this entry entitled "Reporting Vulnerabilities is for the Brave." (Meunier, 2006) Dr. Meunier now provides guidance to all students taking his class after one of his students found vulnerabilities in a site on campus that was eventually exploited. The student and Dr. Meunier had some rather unflattering engagements with the FBI over the alleged hack. The guidance follows:

- *If you find strange behaviors that may indicate that a web site is vulnerable, don't try to confirm if it's actually vulnerable.*

- *Try to avoid using that system as much as is reasonable.*
- *Don't tell anyone (including me), don't try to impress anyone, don't brag that you're smart because you found an issue, and don't make innuendos. However much I wish I could, I can't keep your anonymity and protect you from police questioning (where you may incriminate yourself), a police investigation gone awry and miscarriages of justice. We all want to do the right thing, and help people we perceive as in danger. However, you shouldn't help when it puts you at the same or greater risk. The risk of being accused of felonies and having to defend yourself in court (as if you had the money to hire a lawyer — you're a student!) is just too high. Moreover, this is a web site, an application; real people are not in physical danger. Forget about it.*
- *Delete any evidence that you knew about this problem. You are not responsible for that web site, it's not your problem — you have no reason to keep any such evidence. Go on with your life.*
- *If you decide to report it against my advice, don't tell or ask me anything about it. I've exhausted my limited pool of bravery — as other people would put it, I've experienced a chilling effect. Despite the possible benefits to the university and society at large, I'm intimidated by the possible consequences to my career, bank account and sanity. I agree with HD Moore, as far as*

*production web sites are concerned: "There is no
way to report vulnerability safely".*

It is rather disappointing to read through this and
understand why you would write and stand behind such a
series of guidelines (unless of course you yourself have
experienced such a grilling and the level of intimidation
that comes with it).

Take the recent case of Robert Maley, the former CISO
for the State of Pennsylvania. Robert was fired for
violating an order not to speak about anything related to
the state. He was supposed to get explicit permission
first but decided anyway to divulge some of the
information about a PennDOT incident. He was muzzled
in essence with a gag order not to talk about anything.
To get to the RSA Conference in San Francisco, Robert
too vacation and paid his own freight. Sitting on a panel,
he spoke of the vulnerabilities in this one application.
Not uncommon for security professionals to do at this
conference and not the only security professional
'spanked' for speaking at the conference in 2010.
(Another such security professional was banned from
further speaking events after being quoted in the news
about how he had to learn how to work within his firms
boundaries and culture. He received this ban while at the
conference just prior to his next seminar via email.)

What is unusual about the Maley case is that all the
information he divulged at the conference was already
available in press releases and as a matter of public

record. Yet he was terminated upon return from the conference. In fact, his vacation request that was approved, was now canceled. He was then absent without leave (AWOL) and terminated. (If you don't like the message ...). Apparently, retroactive cancellation of vacation requests, while in progress, is okay in Pennsylvania. It begs the question: Why is it appropriate for Robert Maley to get fired for his infraction yet CEOs and other executives of many firms previously discussed and those in the news today survive with a slap on the hand? When and if they are terminated, their golden parachute awaits.

Back to the VP and his new org. It is obvious that the new VP at this firm has established appropriate levels within guidelines as established by those above him. If not established by those above him then fully agreed upon as part of the annual planning that takes place for internal audit activities and targets. Such a program ensures the illusion of due diligence within this highly important function of this public company. It most importantly ensures the risk is managed and costs are kept very low.

Threats to those finding vulnerabilities continue on a daily basis as I can attest to this. Recently during a two-hour seminar provided at Northeastern University in Boston to a graduate class I was approached by a student with such a dilemma as that described in the Dr. Meunier incident. The student works for a very large financial services firm about to deploy a new web service that gathers information from multiple sites, some sensitive some not. The issue at hand is that in his opinion based upon his technical knowledge as a developer, there are significant vulnerabilities in at least the architecture of the web service. What compounds the issue is that this gentleman has only been employed by this firm for a short two weeks. Imagine what is found after several months and the moral dilemma he will face? The advice I gave him was to tread lightly and explore the whole of the web service; the intent; the design; and do nothing more at this point than to ask non-threatening questions within the scope of his pay grade and level of responsibility. The question I asked myself as I drove home yesterday is 'what would I be doing if I was in his shoes?" Knowing myself as well as anyone can, I know I would dig until I had a full understanding of all issues associated with the web service in question including hard evidence. Of course, I am not in his shoes (this time).

The reporting level of the CISO or corresponding position has direct correlation to the effectiveness with which that individual can execute his/her duties. The position should be as high as possible in the corporate hierarchy. Many organizations bury their security organizations a layer or two within the IT department still viewing information security as a technology issue. When buried two layers down and reporting to IT functional management (such as a VP of infrastructure) like many companies including some very large financial services firms, you find that there is a complete lack of executive awareness or support. It is the worst of all possible worlds. This type of organizational structure for security indicates a serious disregard for the importance of information security and associated risks. It fully strips the CISO of any power or authority, even within IT. The organization is there and there is funding but the illusion that there is any sort of real authority to execute and be heard is predominant. Other organizations have the security function reporting two layers down but to the CTO. In this organizational structure, security is treated as a technology issue with disregard for the behavioral and cultural dimensions of the role and organization. Again, there is very limited power and authority outside of IT and within IT, security takes a back seat to technology and any revenue generating activities. Some organizations have the CISO reporting into the CIO. While this is moving up the value chain, the inherent conflicts between the CISO and CIO will become apparent in times of regulatory stress, vulnerability identification and remediation and/or incidents that involve reputational issues. It is also apparent on a daily basis since the CIO is paid to introduce new technologies which by definition means new threats and vulnerabilities, while the CISO is paid to reduce risk. You will have a reasonable amount of authority within IT as well as executive attention in most cases with this type of organizational structure. Information security in this structure can still be projected as an IT only issue. There is limited power and authority outside of IT. This can cause the CISO to extend his/her reach into the business by building relationships and allies. This is something any and all CISO's should do regardless of the organizational structure (if allowed).

The concept of the chief risk officer is starting to take hold in many organizations where information security is viewed as business risk and assessed against other such business risk such as operational and/or credit risk (should that be the type of organization you are in). This can be seen as the optimum solution for many organizations. There is very good executive exposure and alignment with other risk management functions. It provides power and authority throughout the business with the proper visibility and attention deserved of the role and its value to the business. Unfortunately, this is still fledgling in the information security industry. One such risk in this organizational structure can be the chief risk officer's lack of understanding of information security as a risk management discipline and how to fit it into his/her portfolio of risk groups. This can be overcome through education and support by the CISO and the removal of IT jargon, acronyms and technical terms from presentations and metrics while aligning the deliverables to business risk and impact to the business units. This structure ensures the proper level of due diligence. Some words of warning for reporting to the CRO. It can result in lack of attention to immature security technologies if the position is not tied to the technology infrastructure and operational issues. There can be a disconnect with IT infrastructure developments and application security requirements. There can be resentment from IT that may see this as an ivory tower type position unless the CISO maintains the personal touch to IT and all relative elements.

The final reporting structures can be that of direct CEO/board reporting or to an audit committee/risk management committee function. This does provide for the requisite level of executive attention and control and gives the proper visibility, power and authority across all business units. Such a structure may be optimal in a rapid building or rebuilding effort or in the case of cleanup efforts after a data breach. Many companies have experienced data breaches. Having this type of attention during a set period of time for the reputation rebuilding effort can be very effective. I would suggest using some of this time to establish a follow-on organization that drives the chief risk officer type structure once the dust has settled.

One final item to remember about reporting structures, a change in structure before it's time is not a good idea. All parties must be on the same page, aware of all roles and responsibilities and sign-up for the organizational change. Without this, change will occur but the walls will remain and actually grow higher and thicker. I have seen IT add their own technology risk staff to provide a single point of contact to information security once security was removed from IT. This served to shield IT directly from the information security function ensure a healthy dose of perception management was applied to the newly minted technology risk employees.

Don't Mess with the Cook Until After You've Eaten the Meal

I had the opportunity to interview for a position with a very prestigious Fortune 500 Firm who will remain unnamed. I was a bit hesitant to go to the interview but the opportunity sounded like it could be something I could sink my teeth into. Upon return from the interview, I had time to reflect on the conversations that took place and a couple of issues with organizational structure, title, and level of visibility for the slot. Keep in mind that at the time I was about to be unemployed but I found it necessary to maintain my integrity by being completely honest in my response to the recruiter. This honesty of course will not endear me to the recruiter nor will I be invited (I strongly suspected) to the second round. I authored an email back to the executive recruiter that is more like management consulting advice but one I sent nonetheless:

> *I want to express my sincere appreciation to you and to Fortune 500 Firm as a whole for having me in to interview for the senior corporate infosec person not titled as a CISO position. I was able to gain valuable insights into the role, the responsibilities and where Fortune 500 Firm is with respect to information security, assurance and risk. Please thank Hiring Manager for the opportunity to speak with him and for his candor*

about the role. I am genuinely interested in information security at Fortune 500 Firm.

You had asked me prior to my departure if I had any reservations relative to what I had learned for this position, and I had answered none. During the flight and drive home yesterday I was able to reflect on the discussions we had. There are a couple of items I would like to address.

Fortune 500 Firm has had two people in the role since the 2003 timeframe with this new hire being the third. This does give me some pause as to the true understanding of information security at Fortune 500 Firm, the importance and the proper stature. Organizationally, the reporting structure as presented places the senior corporate infosec person not titled as CISO and true information security expert, four layers below the CIO within information technology. Having been a CISO now for nearly six years, I can safely say from direct experience that this is a tactical placement that will place the selected candidate in a position of weakness. What I mean by that is that the authority of the senior most security position in any Fortune 1000 firm needs to be on par with that of a CIO. The current structure would not afford the selected candidate a valid opportunity to affect change or to execute strategically in a way required of such a prestigious firm as Fortune 500 Firm. The number of regulatory pressures and intensity to safeguard and protect information of various types and sensitivities requires the senior most information security role to be elevated to one of proper authority and position in order to be successful both internally and with external regulatory agencies and audit bodies. It is a very serious role that impacts the company on multiple levels. I believe you are in fact looking for a chief information security officer, someone with the experience, qualifications and moxie to successfully implement security risk in a highly complex culture. Organizational positioning is critical.

The other item I would like to share with you relates to title. Although this may seem trite, my industry experience tells me that another factor in proper position and authority is ensuring the senior most information security person is properly titled as either a CSO or CISO. Having been in this role myself for nearly six years and having earned my stripes as evidenced by the awards and accolades received based upon execution, coming in as a senior corporate infosec person not titled as CISO is not the direction I prefer to take my career. I have proven my skill and security prowess and believe this should be strongly considered.

Starting a new role from a disadvantaged position can be much more challenging than required. When properly placed and titled with full C-level suite support and acknowledgement, any role can hit the ground running when occupied by an experienced industry professional.

Please accept my comments as an expression of continued interest and also of areas for discussion should I still be considered. I realize the gravity of my comments but must make them in order to fully articulate my position honestly and with integrity.

Again, I thank you for the opportunity to interview for the position.

As you can imagine, I did not get a reply. In most cases, they will not take this to heart but will instead think ill of me for sending it. Maybe it was a bit too strong? I could have continued with the process if they invited me to the second and final round without speaking up about the issues as I see them but to do so would have been a deception both to Fortune 500 Firm and me. In any case, I have suffered this type of positioning in the past and do not wish to again find myself in such a predicament. The type of position I seek is the CSO or CISO role with organizational placement that is proper. Either a corporate role or a senior role within a security vendor organization.

Some might say I am an elitist with attitude. I would say until you know my background and the professional situations I have been in (as described in this book), you cannot understand why I would respond in such a way.

Why in God's name would I want to go back to a structure like this one? What is the definition of insanity? Doing the same thing over and over again expecting a different outcome than the previous? Any organization under the regulatory pressures, lawsuits and other statutory scrutiny that this one is should elevate the role to the proper level. As a matter of fact, the role used to be elevated and did have the CISO title. Why in times like these would they revert to burying information security within IT under a novice security professional (although he does have significant IT experience) and not even mention security anywhere in the title? This is an illusion of due diligence.

The hiring manager seemed solid but this was his first foray into information security having just been named the global head for information security a scant four weeks ago (of which two have been vacation). Prior to this, his role was in storage and networking. What struggles would I face reporting to this gentleman? What struggles would he face trying to sell something that he does not fully understand nor grasp? I know what he would face and having been at the firm for more than 15 years, he would accept the negative responses from his superiors and walk away ensuring he would not jeopardize his standing. I would have been left watching significant risk go unattended and again holding the bag should the weight of the risk crush the weak information security and risk infrastructure.

What if I was offered the job and took it only to leave a few months later when a better opportunity came about? Would that be ethical? I don't believe so. Beggars can't be choosers but in this case, professional ethics won out. What would you have done? Maybe in a few more months while still on the street, I might have bent under the pressure to take the job. Maybe not. I really don't wish to find out but for this one, it is best I walk away and I did.

Innocent Until Investigated

Wikipedia defines the presumption of innocence as a legal right that no person shall be considered guilty until finally convicted by a court. The burden of proof is thus on the prosecution, which has to convince the court that the accused is guilty beyond a reasonable doubt. In principle, the defense does not have to 'prove' anything. However, the defense may present evidence tending to show that there is a doubt as to the guilt of the accused.

Conversely, in many authoritarian regimes the prosecution case is, in practice, believed by default unless the accused can prove he is innocent, a practice called presumption of guilt. Many people believe that presumption of guilt is unfair and even immoral because it allows the strategic targeting of any individual, since it's often difficult to firmly establish proof of innocence (for example, it's often impossible to establish an alibi if the person is home alone at the time of the crime).

What you find in many corporations is the practice called presumption of guilt. Character assassination, rumor mongering, or targeting of individuals because they do not flow with the corporate culture or for some other reason, and I speak from experience as described in a previous chapter, perform their job well, beyond the understanding of those in power. The presumption of guilt method is frequently used to discredit the messenger of some bad news. If you don't like the message, discredit the messenger. This is common practice in corporations and government. Just ask Valerie Plame. When those in power don't like a piece of information, they do everything possible to discredit the messenger there by discrediting the message based upon weakness of character or some other personality flaw or action.

This ensures proper perception management continues to reign supreme. Cynical you may think. Practical experience in multiple industries and basic corporate life lessons tells me otherwise. It is how it is done.

Let's move onto perception management. I have alluded to this throughout certain passages of this book. According to Wikipedia, perception management is the actions to convey and/or deny selected information and indicators to influence the intended recipient's emotions, motives, and objective reasoning and drive their official actions favorable to the originator's objectives (Wikipedia, 2010). It is an effective way to steer opinion away from the facts. It is also effective in projecting an image based upon half-truths and outright falsehoods.

In various ways, perception management combines truth projection, operations security, cover and deception, and psychological operations. It is in fact used in civil affairs groups in the military as well as special operations units to sway local populations to a different way of thinking and acting.

Perception management firms exist to sway the market towards marketing messages a firm may wish to convey. The phrase "perception management" has been characterized as a "euphemism" for "an aspect of information warfare." Perception management does involve falsehood and deception, which are important ingredients of perception management. The real purpose is to get the other side to believe what one wishes it to believe, whatever the truth may be.

When used within corporations as a tool against information security and risk, which most who use perception management would say is an outrage to even consider such a practice (which unto itself is part of the program), it is highly effective tool that manages the message and puts infosec professionals on the constant defensive. Already struggling to gain or maintain a seat at the table, infosec professionals continue to fight against cultural norms. Shooting the messenger is an easy way to dispose of the perceived opposition and serves as a warning to others not to tread in these waters.

Regardless the situation, as soon as you are investigated you are no longer innocent. Those in senior level positions have passed down the edict that you, yes you, are guilty of some treasonous act such as the conspiracy to commit security.

One last observation I have cobbled together over the years is the along the lines of 'The best make up the cream that flows to the top.' The observation I have seen and continue to see on a regular basis is a take-off on this topic but a bit different. As I see it, we have grown to accept that mediocrity is the cream of the crop only mediocrity is the cream that jells in the middle. This jelling of mediocrity acts to secure its position and status in corporations acting as a cohesive unit during times of stress ensuring survivability of the jell. Anything to the north or south of the middle is cast aside as unworthy to join the swelling ranks of complacent mediocrity and seen as a direct threat to the well being and sustainability of the masses. My word of warning here is if you are in not in the middle you will be at risk. If you are in the middle, you will not realize it. Mediocrity has become the corporate ruling class rife with ethical anomalies. Beware! You will have to interface with this slow moving mass on a regular basis. Feed it as you must but do not stand in its path as you will be absorbed much like the Borg and a collective consciousness or groupthink. Ayn Rand would be appalled at corporations today surely rebelling against their perception management characterized by the highly constipated stuff shirts who preach a false corporate altruism from a bully pulpit.

If In Doubt...

The Code of Conduct is intended to communicate the Company's high standards of behavior and ethical business practices, which are expected of all employees. Each of us, no matter what our role or job, will eventually have to make choices about right or wrong business conduct. There may be situations where you are uncertain about the legal or ethical course or about whether a business practice or transaction is ethical. As you consider a particular situation, ask yourself these questions:

- Is my action or the action of a co-worker consistent with approved Company practices?
- Can I defend my action to my supervisor, other employees and to the general public?
- Could I comfortably explain my action if it was reported in the newspaper?
- Does my action meet my personal code of behavior?
- Does my action or the action of a co-worker conform to the spirit and guidelines of the Code of Conduct or other Company policies?

A question I have is maybe we are giving the Code of Conduct too much respect? Should we change much of the terminology found in the Code of Conduct to reflect the realities of the corporate world? May we should add some of the following acronyms and use them freely throughout the document[9]:

QFT	Quoted For Truth
DARFC	Duck and run for cover
RISK	Really insignificant security knowledge
BOHICA	Bend over here it comes again
FIDO	F it, drive on
AFCPS	Any fool can plainly see
MBUC	Mind bogglingly unlikely coincidence
BFMI	Brute force and massive ignorance
TNLNSL	Took nothing, left nothing, signed logbook
BMTIPG	Brilliant minds think in parallel gutters
JAFO	Just another freakin' observer
CISO	Completely innocuous silly officer
IKYBYUWYTISBINSYR TWYHINWIM	I know you believe you understand what you think I said, but I'm not sure you realize that what you heard is not what I meant
IHNNKLTIDKN	I have never not known less than I don't know now

---

[9] http://www.gaarde.org/Acronyms/

If you find you are having adverse reactions to the Code of Conduct based upon the words of this document (a document without the acronyms above) and the actual actions of those at the top, review the below warning for Code of Conduct side effects:

- You may have changes in behavior, hostility, agitation, depressed mood, suicidal thoughts or actions while adhering to the corporate Code of Conduct, which may be a MBUC. You may develop these symptoms when you begin reading the document, or develop them after several weeks of employment. If you notice agitation, hostility, depression, or changes in behavior, thinking, or mood that are not typical for you, or you develop suicidal thoughts or actions, anxiety, panic, aggression, anger, mania, abnormal sensations, hallucinations, paranoia, or confusion, destroy the Code, DARFC and resign. Don't wait to become JAFO. Tell your psychiatrist about any history of managerial oppression, lying or other unethical situations before reading the Code, as these actions may worsen while under its control.
- Some people can have allergic reactions to the Code and include: swelling of the face, mouth, and throat that can cause trouble breathing. If you have these symptoms, resign and get medical attention right away. You may find that you have irritable bowel syndrome and uncontrollable flatulence. AFCPS, that there is no cure for this other than resignation.

- The most common side effects include nausea (30%), sleep problems, constipation, gas, and/or vomiting and you may have trouble sleeping, vivid, unusual, or strange dreams while under the influence of the Code. Use caution driving or operating machinery until you know how the Code may affect you. BFMI will not help you in Code adherence.

- Before adhering to the Code, tell your psychiatrist if you have integrity, plan to obtain integrity, or if you have an idealistic view of corporate behaviors.

Unsavory Behaviors

When you look at all the situations I have been in over the years, you may wonder if I have an internal magnet that attracts unsavory behaviors. Something in my personality that is predisposed to delve into unsavory behaviors as deeply as possible almost like an archaeological dig, carefully sifting away each granule of sand, each layer of earth deposited well beyond the surface discovery of the skeleton, but a full excavation of the site; several feet to each side and well below the skeletons deepest bone structure. Applying this method can be timely and tedious as well as dangerous. As you have read throughout this book, there are mines buried throughout the skeletal structure and sometimes the mines are at or just below the surface long before you even discover something to excavate. Such is the life of a security professional in today's corporate and government organizations. We are plagued by improvised explosive devices (IEDs) carefully hidden and obfuscated by leaders at every level of the organization. Mostly by those at the top of the food chain.

When I examine the past trying to rise above the frays looking back and down upon significant accomplishments and equally significant carnage, my vision becomes 20/20 as any Monday morning armchair quarterback has the luxury. In this case, I know there are things I should have done that I did not do; things I should have said that I did not say; actions I took that I should not have taken and words I said that I should not have uttered. Ah yes, the benefits of time to examine, analyze and create a historical record as well as critical definitions of why something happened when it did as a method of rationalization.

What I can safely say without bias is that I survived each situation although not without my scars. I truly hope I have gained the knowledge and wisdom that comes with experience. I do hope that the writings throughout this book serve as a warning to information security and risk professionals as well as anyone working in public and private entities, that nefarious activities do take place on a regular basis. All you need to do is look. What you will want to know and fully understand is how deep do 'they' want you to look? This is a critical point in your survival. If you are asked to dig down a foot, only go 11 inches. I also hope that throughout your reading, you too have gained awareness and knowledge learning ways to avoid the pitfalls associated with my career to this point.

Information security is still an immature profession as evidenced by my everyday interactions with business leaders, peers, IT professionals, legal departments, internal audit and most any group associated with risk. In some instances, it is much like Jack Nicholson's statements in A Few Good Men when he exhorts:

"… and my existence, even though grotesque to you … you need me on that wall, you want me on that wall …"

The information security and risk profession is not only a military-type insurance policy that serves to protect and defend against intruders foreign and national alike, but a necessary tool required by all organizations that needs a visible and viable seat at the table of leadership. Let me correct that. Information security is not an insurance policy at all. Insurance policies are taken out because you know you are going to die and they offer nothing to improve your life. Over time, insurance policies have their deductible increased and coverage reduced. I know this is not what CISOs want.

I sometimes ask myself, what if I had a seat at the table in some of these organizations and was able to speak freely and openly about the threats, vulnerabilities, risks, impacts, likelihoods, ethical issues, and true business risk without having to use fear, uncertainty and doubt (FUD) as I define it? Would the same issues have occurred? Would the same stress have manifested itself as it did?

Is FUD really something that should not be used? In my opinion, FUD is a necessary tool in the toolbox. The US Government uses it on a regular basis. Marketing in TV ads, printed material, and radio use fear to sell. IT vendors use FUD to sell. CIOs use FUD to secure extra funding. Business leaders use FUD to justify mergers and acquisitions. Politicians use FUD to get their bills passed into law. Teachers use FUD as do parents to motivate their students and children. It is inherent in most everything we do. Why would we want to remove this effective tool from our toolbox? We would not. We do need to place a warning on usage that states frequent use will cause a 'cry wolf' effect whereby responsiveness will cease. It is much like repeated beatings about the head and shoulders that will result in injury and even death. Timely and very limited usage coupled with solid metrics can be quite effective.

So what will you do when ethical behavior, integrity, corporate due diligence and attorney client privilege collide in a cacophony of opinion and negligence? How will you survive when you find yourself in the absolute middle of this vortex? Information security and risk professionals need to persevere and press on. We are a fine bunch of soldiers that will always be under fire. We must maintain our integrity and we must above all execute to the highest ethical standards. As soon as we compromise our position, we have failed. I have seen security officers who have in fact lost their way. They become *exception rubber stamps* ignoring the risks that flow unchecked during their watch. They give our profession a bad name yet continue to operate under the guise of the arsonist calling in the fire. They are excellent during incidents as they take operational command even when the procedure calls for others to do so, but beyond this, most fall back to their comfort zone. They do not reflect the ethos we signed up for when becoming CISSPs and CISMs. In many cases, they did so as a method for continued employment. Information security and risk professionals are just that, professionals. We are in a profession and as such, we must maintain our objectivity and personal and professional integrity. This is the core tenet of any information security professional. We do not have to fall prey to the idea that not breaking our ethos is sign of corporate operational immaturity. It is okay to be accused for conspiracy to commit security. I have had CIOs state this indicating that maturity is doing what is necessary for the company and in many cases what is necessary for the CIO to look good. Any other path shows immaturity and a lack of commitment to the company. This is a method that supports the illusion of due diligence.

I have had discussions with peers in the industry who say you have to consider who pays you and where your paycheck originates in your decisions. Of course you must consider this but your job is to identify the risk; quantify the risk; provide remediation and protection strategies as well as recommended safeguards, document the need for funding, provide a roadmap and timeline for completion amongst a host of other business critical risk items, delivering this information to the C-level suite for acknowledgement and inclusion with the rest of the business risk the C-level suite must examine for action or acceptance. If you can get to this level with your message; if you can deliver a cohesive and comprehensive corporate intelligence estimate on the information security and even physical risk associated with your organizations to the C-level suite or even

210

beyond; then know that you have in fact done your job to the best that you are allowed in this day and age. You have nothing to be ashamed about if a breach occurs. You will of course second-guess yourself. If I had only pressed harder. If I had only pushed my message further. This will only eat a hole in your psyche. You need to let it go. Pushing and pressing too hard can lead to threats of or actual termination as I have faced in my career and as you have read about in preceding pages.

I ask you to let the situations and actions taken in the preceding pages digest and sink in. If this book provides information security and risk professionals insights that save them the same fate, that allows them to avoid some of the issues yet solve their problems with integrity and ethical behavior, then I will have succeeded in my efforts as a peer and professional.

Bibliography

Ethics Roll Call, The Institute for Law Enforcement Administration. (2002). Retrieved March 9, 2010, from Ethics Corner: http://www.cailaw.org/ilea/summer02/corner.html

Guthrie, A. (1969, September 29). *A Tribute To Officer Obie.* Retrieved February 20, 2010, from A Tribute To Officer Obie: http://www.arlo.net/obie.shtml

Guthrie, A. (1967). *Lyrics - Alice's Restaurant.* Retrieved February 15, 2010, from The Lyrics Connection: http://www.arlo.net/resources/lyrics/alices.shtml

ISACA. (2010). *ISACA Code of Professional Ethics.* Retrieved April 18, 2010, from Code of Professional Ethics:
http://www.isaca.org/Template.cfm?Section=Home&CONTENTID=55498&TEMPLATE=/ContentManagement/ContentDisplay.cfm

ISC2. (1996). *ISC2 Code of Ethics.* Retrieved April 18, 2010, from ISC2: http://www.isc2.org/ethics/default.aspx

Meunier, P. (2006, May 22). *CERIAS: Reporting Vulnerabilities is for the Brave.* Retrieved June 22, 2008, from CERIAS the center for education and research in information security:

http://www.cerias.purdue.edu/site/blog/post/reporting-vulnerabilities-is-for-the-brave/

Sarbox, M. (2003). *Why Sox Happened*. Retrieved October 10, 2009, from SOX-online: http://www.sox-online.com/according_to_ms_sarbox.html

TRAC. (2009, January 5). *US Code Title 18 Section 912*. Retrieved October 18, 2009, from TRAC: http://trac.syr.edu/laws/18/18USC00912.html

Wikipedia. (2010, April 10). *Perception management - Wikipedia, the free encyclopedia*. Retrieved April 18, 2010, from Perception management: http://en.wikipedia.org/wiki/Perception_management